In the Fullness of Faith

Hans Urs von Balthasar

In the Fullness
of Faith

On the Centrality of the
Distinctively Catholic

Translated by Graham Harrison

Ignatius Press   San Francisco

Title of the German original:
Katholisch
© 1975 Johannes Verlag
Einsiedeln, Switzerland

Cover by Victoria Hoke Lane

With ecclesiastical approval
The granting of the *Imprimatur* does not imply the
acceptance of the theological opinions of the author.

© 1988 Ignatius Press, San Francisco
All rights reserved
ISBN 0–89870–166–x
Library of Congress Catalogue Number 88–80727
Printed in the United States of America

Contents

The reader looking for a loose collection of aspects and perspectives, observations and data without any claim to system and completeness, can find them in the pages of Josef Neuner's "Die Weltkirche. Die Katholizität der Kirche im Missionswerk" (in Holböck-Sartory, Mysterium der Kirche, 1962) or in M.-J. Le Guillou, Mission et Unité, 2 vols. (1960), or in Wolfgang Beinert, Um das dritte Kirchenattribut. Die Katholizität der Kirche, 2 vols. (1964). Or he can turn to a work of genius that marked a breakthrough to new Catholic thought, namely, Henri de Lubac's Catholicism (1936).

Here we are concerned with only those aspects that characterize the mystery of the (Roman) Catholic Church vis-à-vis the other Christian denominations, i.e., things which, in ecumenical dialogue, Catholics are often more reluctant to mention and which they try to play down. There are two ways of doing the reverse, of showing that such things are often central. There is the "counter-Reformation" way of polemics, meeting assertions with counter-assertions; and there is the genuinely Catholic way, which starts out from the mystery affirmed by both parties and endeavors on this basis to show the distinctively Catholic teaching, so that, from his own standpoint, the non-Catholic partner-in-dialogue is able to see the inner connections. This is neither "controversy", therefore, nor diplomatic "irenicism", nor some neutral "comparative study of denominations", but a reflection that can call itself ecumenical because it is Catholic.

9

Foreword

This small book was written as an expression of friendship. The author reached his 70th birthday in 1975. Such anniversaries—in Germanic countries—never pass unnoticed. The more so in this case since Fr. von Balthasar has made so many grateful friends—and not only because of his books—among all Christian groups and beyond. He wanted to respond to all, beyond the more personal expressions of gratitude. And that is the origin of this book whose original title was the single word: *Catholic*.

Catholic: that title perfectly expresses the content, which is simply the explanation of that word. Not a lyrical exaltation, not even, really, a profession of faith. Nor, in the strict sense, a treatise of apologetics or theology. There is no systematic order to it. No hidden polemical agenda, no attempt to be contemporary—though there are reflections scattered throughout which, without direct allusion, flash a brilliant light on the present situation and provide a standard to evaluate ecumenical dialogue. Very simply, the explanation of a word, in measured tones, as from one friend to another who is perhaps startled and wants to understand.

The original circle of friends first intended extends to unknown readers. Look, says the author to each of us, without provocation but without fear. Look at what being a Catholic means to me. But it is not my own imagination that I have consulted—but rather what the Church, spouse of Christ and guardian of the Scriptures, has taught me of herself, by her life as by her word, by her origins, her past, her present. The explanation is directed first of all at Protestants, and more especially, in several passages, Lutherans. But it is also addressed to us all. In fact, it ought to be beneficial above all to Catholics themselves. For we are always in need to learn, to understand better in order to become more fully what we are.

In what pertains to the spirit of this explanation, the original and spontaneous method it follows, these are amply described in the first pages and need no definition here. I will only caution the reader: do not expect a personal testimony or subjective self-revelation. It is not an individual who is speaking. It is a believer, a son of the Church who, with his own personal accent, tells us of the faith to which he has committed himself, and which is the same for all.

Henri de Lubac

Introduction:
The Present Situation

Can People Still Understand the Word "Catholic"?

"Catholic" is a quality. It means totality and universality, and the understanding of it presupposes a particular human attitude of mind and heart. It is true that the catholicity of the Catholic Church is primarily a revelation and communication of the divine totality; it is true that the acceptance of this revelation by men is primarily the work of grace; all the same, it is possible for a historical period to be stretched beyond its limit by this grace. This seems to be the case in the period in which we live.

For us, efficiency resides in the part, in the party; the alternative is a tolerant and inefficient cosmopolitanism. Quality seems to go with the part, the partial; totality seems to be synonymous with a lack of contour. We need to ask ourselves whether a great deal of our ecumenism is not bought by sacrificing quality. (In the ancient world, the *oikumene* was the geographical span of the inhabited world, the "cosmopolis".) Does it not bear some resemblance to the religious syncretism of pre-Christian Rome?

The Catholica is labelled "Roman Catholic", as one clan among others, and it is a source of irritation that the Church refuses to join the World Council of Churches on an equal footing. For the WCC is the kind of totality that is intelligible to people nowadays. Furthermore, the attribute "Catholic" has become subject to so many nuances that every denomination upholding the ancient Creed lays claim to it and interprets it as it thinks best.

One particular claim made by the Catholica can hardly be regarded as valid any more under present conditions, even if it is true that this claim was bound to arouse indignation at every period of history: the Catholica claims to be a special, historico-sociological entity possessing universal relevance. Modern man finds this claim foolish, arrogant and intolerant.

The Whole in the Part

The claim of the Catholica was more readily understood in times governed by a vertically arranged picture of the world. Ours is marked by the scientific approach that, quite legitimately in its own sphere, tries to interpret all phenomena in a horizontal and quantitative manner in order to make them increasingly perspicuous and synthesizable. In contrast, the vertical arrangement means that a whole, the human soul, for instance, can present itself in a plurality of bodily members in such a way that only on the basis of the overall totality can each member exist and be what, in reality, it is, i.e., not a mere machine for holding things, but a human hand. If the hand could think, it would understand itself to be part of the expressive equipment of a totality superior to the members.

This metaphor limps, of course, for the Church's relationship with its animating principle is not that of a member (or even of a whole body) to the spiritual soul. All the same, Paul uses the metaphor as an aid to understanding. We shall deal later with the question of why a truly universal principle should select one particular, terrestrial organ as its (exclusive and inclusive) means of expression.

Here, initially, we are concerned only to show that a ("hierarchically") superordinate reality can so inform a subordinate plurality that the latter is lifted up into the former's unity without being robbed of its distinctive character. Thus a formative principle seizes on matter and provides itself with a shape. (We must also realize that it may no longer be possible for some people to appreciate this.)

The Church's formative principle remains a divine mystery; ultimately it can only be believed: God, present in a man, Jesus Christ, in such a way that the latter represents the whole of mankind in a real and effectual manner, reconciling the world to God through his cross and Resurrection. This leads us into the darkness: What is really happening on that cross? What is he suffering and undergoing there? (For no one has ever been able to tell.) And how is the Church interiorly affected by these events? (For "I am crucified with Christ", and "you are risen with Christ".) The Church does not associate herself with these events on her own initiative; on the contrary, it is they that make her what she is. (But no one can put this into words either.) The Catholica exists only by believing the mystery of which it is the expression and by endeavoring to correspond to it and testify to it in word and life. The measure of its catholicity, which permeates and informs it, is found, not in itself, but above it, in the mystery of Christ. But in turn this mystery cannot be isolated from the testimony of the Catholica.

A Testimony Unworthy of Belief

The testimony of the Catholica is deeply hidden, as deep as the mystery to which it testifies. Ask any member of the more educated classes in the West or the East what he understands by "Catholic", what he associates with it: the Inquisition, the Pill, and suchlike. In what is her weakest conciliar document, the Church has "given a blessing" to the mass media, but can she make use of these media to unveil her most fundamental mystery, the only thing that can make her believable, to every Tom, Dick or Harry? Isn't it inevitable that, in such a context, she will have to present herself, at best, in a secondary, more morality-based, more "catchy" form, at one remove from her reality? But in this case, surely, will she not be engaging in propaganda rather than mission?

At this secondary level the Catholica has implicitly accepted the role of being a "church" or religious body among others. And isn't this simply a matter of fact anyway since, in the course of its history, it has split into many "churches"—pre-Chalcedonian, Orthodox, Reformed, Anglican, etc.—each claiming to give the nearest approximation to a pure witness to the mystery? Unless a person is somehow fascinated by the mystery, he is bound to be put off by these differences, for the Catholica is supposed to be externally identifiable as such: "that ye all may be one, as I and the Father are one".

Within the "Roman Catholic" Church herself there are differences. There are the polarizations in the wake of the Second Vatican Council: left versus right, progressive versus conservative. Some people dissolve allegedly rigid forms until nothing is left but formlessness, while others hold fast to these forms until they actually ossify. Neither is replaced by anything that promises to last, but by things cobbled together in haste, outdated even before they see the light of day. It is hard to say whether this is simply due to our period's inability to create genuine forms or to a specifically Christian inability. How ephemeral is practically all Christian art; how ephemeral practically all Christian music and lyrics nowadays! The Baroque art of the post-Reformation era shows that Christianity did not have to be like this.

The many sects that have split off from the Catholica have all exported some part of its vitality, partly through maintaining authentic tradition and partly by allegedly going back to the origins. In this way they have lent credibility to the idea that there is little left of the Catholic Church but bones without flesh, a skeleton, an institution, an establishment. The Church's internal polarizations heighten this impression: the strength of the extremes indicates that the center, which alone can hold them together, has a grave lack of vitality. Who would believe a testimony that is so polemically splintered when it claims to speak for the totality?

Kenosis?

The water that flowed eastward from under the threshold of the Temple in Ezekiel's vision and eventually became an impassable river began as a trickle. Similarly, not more than a few drops came from the wound in the side of Jesus. Should the river of the Catholica return to the formlessness of its origin in order to regenerate itself? And in the meantime must its witness become a silent one until it acquires a new and credible form on the basis of a newly won center and mission? Or is all external form to be dismantled?

In the life of Jesus there was a moment when everything stood still, a moment of *peripeteia*. The synoptic writers arrange their entire portrayal around it. It came when the sensation caused by his words and miracles, and the enthusiasm of the masses, had reached saturation point, while the increasing opposition of the leaders was coalescing into the death-sentence. From this moment on, Jesus resolutely "set his face toward Jerusalem", dragging his dismayed disciples after him and well aware of what was in store for him.

Paul experiences this same moment of stillness when, ignoring all the warnings, he sets out for Jerusalem, the Spirit telling him that bonds and hardships await him there.

Why should the hour not strike for the Church too, this decisive hour in world history? Why not today? In that case her descent into the depths should be just as resolute as the Lord's former going up to Jerusalem. Nor need she be spared inner anxiety, for her Lord was acquainted with it. Such anxiety can coincide, in temporal terms, with men's other fear of self-destruction and the annihilation of the phylum that carries them. Perhaps the Church has to accompany mankind on its way to the scaffold; and it may be that mankind has a particular distaste for such a companion nowadays. The brutality of the facts, which so preoccupies mankind, accords ill with any reference to a transcendental truth; indeed, it sounds like pure distraction.

The Transformation of Fear

Fear mercilessly grips the human throat. It fills the psychiatrists' consulting rooms, populates the psychiatric hospitals, increases the suicide figures, lays blast–bombs, sets off cold wars and hot wars. We try to root it out of our souls like weeds, anesthetizing ourselves with optimism, trying to persuade ourselves with a forced philosophy of hope; we make all possible stimulants available, domesticate the nomadic urge by means of the tourist industry; we invite people to engage in every form of self-alienation.

Others preach, from outside, as it were, that we should "simply" trust in Jesus, but such consolation eludes us.

The Catholic reality does not eliminate fear, it transforms it. In the Eucharist and the forgiveness of sins the event of the cross becomes really present; but its fear also becomes present, its fear that gathered up and exceeded all the world's fear. This was a fear that had been offered to God, a fear on our behalf, designed to free the sinner from fear.

Jesus' prophetic words to the Church constantly alternate between terrible facts to which we can only respond in fear—"I send you out as sheep in the midst of wolves" (Mt 10:16)—and words encouraging us to overcome fear because it is God-given: "Let not your hearts be troubled; believe in God, believe also in me" (Jn 14:1); "You will be sorrowful, but your sorrow will turn into joy" (Jn 16:20). The woman cries out when her time for giving birth has come, and the Catholica has to share in her Lord's birth pangs for the world. Nor can the Church's representatives, in particular, expect to be free from anxiety for the Church, whether they be saints on the one hand or officials on the other; they must not try to hide behind their "representational" role. The understandable fear that the Church's testimony could cease to be heard must not lead us to make it even more inaudible by the use of the world's amplification systems. "He will not wrangle or cry aloud, nor will any one hear his voice in the streets" (Mt 12:19). Vociferous theologians and Catholic T.V. personalities are particularly unconvincing nowadays: all they do is to oversimplify things in a way that is quite frightening.

The Church is afraid of having to bare herself in public; this is both a human fear and a fear that comes from the cross. The individual Christian must not be indifferent to this *angst*; he must not dodge it as if it only concerned "experts" and "officials", as if it were only some inconsequential unease on the part of a clergy struggling to discover its "sociological identity".

The Loss of the Corporate Subject

It is only "in company with all the saints" that we can "comprehend what is the breadth and length and height and depth and to know the love of Christ which surpasses knowledge, that you may be filled with all the fullness of God" (Eph 3:18f.). This means that no individual can assess for himself what constitutes Catholic reality. No theologian thinks things out in isolation, and no believer prays, suffers and lives out his life unto himself alone. Any Christian who has experienced this in a vivid way knows that he must cling closely to the Church, must follow and appropriate what she addresses to mind and heart. She alone utters the perfect *Fiat*, she alone is the seat of wisdom; it is when closed and despairing souls penetrate to her center that they can open up.

We are only participants in the Church's spirituality and faith; we drink from it, we live and work within it, and no one can possess it fully. But since, for a hundred reasons, the inherited community bonds are decaying, those people and things which maintain the communal inheritance are getting fewer and fewer. Then we try as far as possible to impose the burden of the whole onto each individual, to squeeze as much as possible into the narrow confines of the individual. This cannot be done, and as a result the content becomes abstract and theoretical, no longer touching our lives, let alone shaping them. In practice, all we do is taste and try a little of this and a little of that, at random. This explains the increasingly evident flatness, the insipid and forced character of the individual Christian life, the worrying preponderance of programs and requirements. There is no longer any participation at root level; everything has to be done and intended deliberately, everything has to be justified, discussed and decided upon. No wonder that nowadays the pedagogic element—not in the purest sense, but strongly tending toward propaganda—predominates in religious matters, imitating the successful methods of secular advertising, with its gimmicks, slogans and clichés, its mass-distribution from some central office. The individual's personal significance has become tiny.

(I. F. Görres)

This loss of the ability to participate in the corporate subject signifies a direct loss of the Catholic instinct, which can only "know" provided that its object "surpasses knowledge". Where this instinct is absent, people settle for what can be known within the parameters of the world. Here there is the danger of an incorrectly understood *aggiornamento* that would reduce itself to the average capacity of "modern man", not believing him capable of the effort required to integrate himself into that subject (the Church) which alone is empowered to give *the* response to the Word. Saints are needed if the Church's language down through the centuries, in its thousand tongues, is to be uttered to modern ears as something dear and familiar (rather than as an unintelligible muttering), and if the "personal opinions" practically everyone has and proclaims nowadays are to be broadened to become views of the Church, Catholic views. This is the only way to bring back those who are "partially identified" with the Church, i.e., who are situated at some distance from the center, that center which lies above and below all the petty inadequacies they keep tripping over.

Dedication

Our times are iconoclastic. The desire to get rid of images embraces far more than icons and statues of the Sacred Heart. It is hostile to all developed forms. The same demolition machines hammer at the walls from inside and outside. Not only the protective ramparts of revelation, but "dogmas" too are reduced to the proportions of reason. Not only is authority (the presence of God in self-revelation) rejected as irreconcilable with the spirit of the age, but the Church's infrastructures too—schools, hospitals, religious houses with the beauty of their ordered lives—are under threat. Perhaps in the future the contemplative monastery really will be called "Gulag".

There are two kinds of dissolution. Seen from afar they seem related in the same way as death and sleep ("Our friend Lazarus is asleep"). Sleep is the withdrawal of all feelers and antennae; we are once more enfolded in life's origin in order to be regenerated ("Unless a man be born again . . ."); we shrink down to that "little remnant" which bears the whole promise. Death is the will for the amorphous and anarchic; sleep is a concentration on the fruit that drops into the furrow, is covered over and released by it, with the promise of a new form and a harvest.

That person has the greatest freedom who can let go of his present form and allow himself to be regenerated in the formless origin, in the nothingness of the seed-cell—his original vocation, which has always remained fresh! Jesus Christ's entire work for the world was present when he, in this seed-like nothingness, let himself be implanted in the Mother's womb by the Holy Spirit, ready and open for every wish that came from the Father: "Behold, I come to do your will." He did not have a plan of work neatly drawn up, but simply harkened to the inner voice, with an overflowing desire to receive and carry out the Father's instructions. The Son was assimilated to the "lowliness" of the "Handmaid" in whom he was now growing. His was an in-difference, a lack of distinction, consisting of pure readiness for God. His life hung on God's will at every moment.

There was another man who specialized in living in this way at every moment: the "pilgrim" who journeyed on the roads between Manresa, Venice, Jerusalem, Paris, England, Loyola, Padua, Rome. A universal molder of men because he himself remained universally pliable, like *materia prima*. He was like a shadow of the kenotic obedience of the Son of God. He was so firmly anchored in the womb that produces all forms that he was not basically disturbed by the de-formation and liquidation of what he had fashioned, even when it was done by his own disciples. He was like the grain of wheat from the Egyptian tombs, ready to sprout after millennia.

To him these untimely fragments are dedicated.

Catholic

Jesus Is Catholic

Jesus must be Catholic, otherwise his Church, which follows him and is promised his fullness, could not be called Catholic. Being Catholic means embracing everything, leaving nothing out. How can an individual human being do this, even if he *is* the only begotten Son of God? We shall not explain this by theological speculation. It is something that can reveal itself to us only if, in the openness of faith, we let our eyes rest on his self-manifestation. He is the revelation of someone else, of the Father, who is "greater" than he, and yet with whom he is "one". This is the message of his words and his life.

He can reveal the Father in this way only through a twofold movement: he steps forward (with divine authority) in order to make the Father visible, and simultaneously he steps back (as the Suffering Servant) in order to reveal the Father, not himself. We must not fail to discern him in his mode of stepping back, for he is the only way to the Father. In other words, the Father reveals himself by revealing the Son; he gives himself by giving his Son: *dando revelat, et revelando dat* (Bernard). Nor must we cling to him in his stepping forth, for, in all the density of his flesh, his whole aim is to be transparent, revealing the heart of God. In the same breath he can say, "My flesh is food indeed" and "It is the spirit that gives life, the flesh is of no avail." We must not hedge him round with a pietistic Jesus-spirituality on the grounds that "only the Son knows the Father"; he is the Door, and a door is not for clinging to: it is for going through. He is "the way": we are not meant to stand still on it but walk along it, toward "my Father's house", which has "many rooms". And at the same time we do not leave these rooms and this path behind us, for Jesus is also the light of the world, the truth, the Resurrection, the presence of eternal life. But he is these things, not in his own power, but because he manifests the Father's love.

Lest we become completely confused and wearied by this riddle of his simultaneous stepping forward and stepping back, his appearances and disappearances, he goes beyond it: when he rises from the dead and goes back to the Father, he sends the Holy Spirit from the Father. This Holy Spirit is the one, whole, personal manifestation and confirmation of this baffling unity between Father and Son, the divine "We" that is more than the mere "I" and "Thou". It leads beyond the endless process of counting up, of supplementary definitions, to the reality of mutual presence and indwelling, without causing Father and Son to submerge in the Spirit. The Spirit comes to the aid of our helplessness in the face of the unity of opposites so clearly expressed in the gospel. He rewards us for not trying to resolve this apparent contradiction by our own efforts—for this would be to destroy the core of the Catholic reality: if we are to see things properly, we must include the opposite of what we have seen. It is not that what we see suddenly turns ("dialectically") into its opposite, but that in the lowliness of Jesus there is a direct revelation of his lofty nature; that in his severity we discern his mercy, etc. And it is not that, in his human lowliness, he shows the greatness of the divine Father; it is not that his human severity prepares the way for the Father's compassion. Rather, his lowliness reveals the humiliation of the Father's love, and *that* shows his greatness. Thus, too, his human severity reveals the unshakable nature of the Father's love, and hence of its compassion. So, in the distinction between Father and Son, we discern simultaneously the unity of the divine essence, and, within it, the possibility of uniting those qualities that seem to us irreconcilable. The famous Catholic "and"—Scripture "and" Tradition, etc.—which is the object of Protestant criticism, has its true origin here, and here alone. A Church can be Catholic only because God is Catholic first, and because, in Jesus Christ and ultimately in the Holy Spirit, this catholicity on God's part has opened itself to the world, simultaneously revealing and giving itself. The Spirit is "Person", the "We" in God: he provides the basis for the "we" that exists between God and ourselves, and hence too between men. But we would know and possess nothing of this if Jesus Christ had not stood at the alpha and omega of all God's ways in the world, as the form of revelation available to anyone who is open to it, i.e., is prepared to believe.

The Spirit Proves . . . What Is Beyond Proof

The Spirit's chief quality, in obediently allowing himself to be sent out into the world by Father and Son, is his freedom. He blows whither he will and cannot be fixed in any particular form. He appears as a hovering presence (the "dove"), communication ("tongues"), devouring transformation ("flame"), a breeze that allows us to breathe deeply ("wind"). He "interprets" the mysterious figure of Jesus, revealing its divine being, its trinitarian dimensions, its mystery-quality; in this way the Spirit proves and "convicts" (Jn 16:8). He withdraws Jesus from all rationalistic incursions, and he also prevents Scripture (which he inspired), dogma (which interprets) and the Church's discipline from being swallowed up in purely worldly categories. He lends his wings to the Woman of the Apocalypse so that she may flee to the desert.

He refuses to let himself be caught and domesticated, not even by pneumatic "methods" of prayer. We must not cling to Jesus, but let him ascend "to my Father and your Father"; only if we exhibit a readiness that stipulates no conditions can the Spirit, in his freedom, prove to us that the entire Catholic revelation—God, Christ, the Church—was and remains a project undertaken by the sovereign free love of God.

God's Love Is Catholic

God's love is ever greater; we can never catch up with it. It has no other ground but itself. It comes to us from ever further afield and goes forth to embrace wider vistas than I could ever imagine. That is why, in my limitedness, I always have to add an "and"; but what I thus "add" has always been there in the love of God.

When God, in sovereign freedom, enters into a world, he is not doing something else, something additional (as if God were Catholic in himself and became even more Catholic by bringing what is not-God, creation, into his totality); the Father of Jesus Christ is never any other than the Creator, who, showing them great care, carries all his creatures in his bosom. Everything temporal has its place within God's eternity.

The Incarnation is not an episode in the life of God: the Lamb is slain from all eternity, and hence was born, grew up, and rose again from all eternity too. In itself, the adopting of human nature, with all its ignorance and limitation, into the divine nature is not an event in time, although the human nature so adopted, like ours, was something living and dying in time.

(C. S. Lewis)

Furthermore, the process of integrating creation into God's world (and within the time-dimension it really is a process: the lost sheep is searched for, carried home and put back into the flock) is always present in God's plan of salvation (cf. Eph 1:1–10) as a complete design; it is carried out in a sequence that is unbreakable (cf. Rom 8:29f.) and in which neither human nor divine freedom is overplayed.

At the beginning there stands the "and" in "God *and* the world". In its abstractness, in this context of juxtaposition, however, it would not be a Catholic "and" unless it were contained, right from the outset, in the concrete "hyphen" represented by the incarnate Son (and he is more than a mere "mediator" between two parties: he is the One who creates unity: Gal 3:20) and the sending of the Holy Spirit, who brings everything to a conclusion (yet definitively opens everything up), enabling the creature to participate in the "divine nature" (2 Pet 1:4) as well as embracing it—as the divine "We"—in the community of the Trinity.

This community cannot perfect itself apart from the mutual presence to one another of the divine Persons; equally, it cannot do without the reciprocity of God and his creature if it is to show forth its precious richness.

Just as this catholicity goes beyond a dialectic of reversed opposites, it also goes beyond a *coincidentia oppositorum*. Rather, it is an *inclusion*: nature is included in grace, the sinner is included in forgiving love, and all plans and purposes are included in a supreme *gratis*—"for nothing".

Catholicity and Salvation History

Now let us turn to the other side. What has always been present in God's designs and God's eternity must become a historical reality in time. Jesus' catholicity is not only "vertical", as it were, doing God's will on earth as in Heaven and revealing God in the world: it is also "horizontal", recapitulating the history of Adam's race (to use Irenaeus' magnificent expression).

It has been said, not unjustly, that Jesus of Nazareth said nothing new. The elements of his teaching lie before us like uncut stones ready for construction, indeed, often like cut stones. The only new thing he brought (again to borrow from Irenaeus) was himself, but thus he brought with him *omnem novitatem*. As a result of his fate, his cross and Resurrection, the Jewish *berakah* becomes the Eucharist. So (in Luke as in John) he can say in all truth that Moses and the prophets, or that the law and the prophets and the Psalms, spoke of him, and that Abraham, looking ahead, beheld his day and gave his Yes to God. He understands himself to be history's point of convergence, the fullness, the integration; he is the reason why, from the beginning, there has been a commerce, an "and" between God and the world.

For where God's Son becomes "flesh", that is, man, the whole world is involved, not exclusively the history of Israel. For man himself is the epitome of the cosmos. Thus, when this unique man has completed his course, the gospel will have to be "proclaimed to all creatures"; the "dividing wall of hostility" between particular and universal salvation history has been broken down, and the only "law" valid henceforward is the "law of Christ" (Gal 6:2). This law prescribes, without any qualification, "Bear ye one another's burdens", since One has carried the burden of all. In fulfilling the Old Covenant the promised Messiah fulfills far more: he fulfills the "desire of all nations". This is the only way, in terms of history, that the fulfillment is Catholic. (This is why the covenant with Noah precedes that with Abraham.)

The Messiah's catholicity, however, is not the sum of additions ("and" plus "and" plus "and"): it is fullness in advance. Because it embraces everything, the partial aspects can find their place within it ("Before Abraham was, I am"). This does not mean that the parts do not matter to the whole: on the contrary, they are essential to it if it is to *be* the fullness (recapitulating the world in itself), taking up all that is fragmentary and hence tragic and giving it a finally redeemed and un-tragic place in God's totality, in which there are "many rooms".

Furthermore, the full-fillment of the Old Covenant means that the fullness of Christ can be spelled out for the future—for the Church's history—in a totally new way. As Henri de Lubac has shown, the entire theological exegesis of Scripture, from the beginning up to modern times, was a ceaseless re-interpretation the "words" of the Old Covenant in the new sense, the new "sentence", provided by Jesus Christ. The sentence goes beyond the words that form it, but the words explain the sentence. And since the catholicity of Christ is the evident and fundamental phenomenon of the New Covenant, it can be interpreted in a broader and broader sense (and this applies to the words of the Old Covenant too). Throughout the whole history of the Church, of the saints, of dogma, each new interpretation can be verified by referring it to the fundamental deposit.

In its Catholic "fullness" the fundamental phenomenon is interpreted by the Holy Spirit, and the Scriptures of the New Covenant are a normative part of this interpretation. Theologically speaking, therefore, it is irrelevant to introduce a dichotomy between Jesus' words and deeds uttered and performed before people who were not yet Christian believers, and such words and deeds as perceived with the eyes and ears of the Church's post-Easter faith. The primal phenomenon is the Whole: the Word of God, perceived and heard by the power of the Holy Spirit, Christ together with his Church.

The Cross as the Center of Catholic Reality

How can those who come afterward put their feet into the "footprints" of him who followed a unique and inimitable path? Before tackling this difficult problem it can be helpful to consider that, in a certain sense, Jesus saw his path as an imitation, a following, of the rejected ambassadors God had already sent to Israel (indeed, according to the Letter to the Hebrews, of all those who had trusted and suffered before him). Not as if he stands at the same level, but his all-embracing suffering takes into itself their particular suffering—and their faith, which is always a renunciation and hence a suffering. He who is unique, of one time, has an inner knowledge of what is of all times; not only a knowledge of the sins of all, with which the Crucified is laden, but also a knowledge of all the more or less successful or failed attempts people make to follow the path of God's call.

The primitive Church interpreted the destiny of Jesus primarily according to the prophecy of the Suffering Servant (Is 52–53), who was raised up because of his suffering on behalf of others. This contains at least the suggestion that, in the cross of Christ, the manifold sufferings of the people of old (and, behind them, of the heathen too—Job!) are drawn up into the catholicity of the cross.

In this way, albeit remotely at first, we begin to see a way of discipleship that leads into the future. Somehow this discipleship is an even greater mystery: For is it not the case that, with the cross, everything is already "accomplished" (Jn 19:30)? Surely there is nothing left to be done? We must not exaggerate this paradox, however: we must not take Jesus' words on discipleship, for instance, as something given that needs no further interpretation. Rather, it is only when we meet this paradox that the central meaning of the word "Catholic" —which is also the meaning most familiar to us—will gradually open up.

The Cross and the Clash of Wills

The believer knows that, on the cross, Jesus "took away the sins of the world". Guilt cannot simply be blown away; it must be expiated; it must be dissolved in the pain of sorrow for sin and the confession of guilt. We have an embryonic grasp of this, even if what happens on the cross ("he was made to be sin"—2 Cor 5:21) remains infinitely mysterious and can only be accepted in faith.

But behind the aspect of guilt there is another aspect, to which less attention is devoted. God has created human beings as individual persons with individual freedom; by nature these freedoms clash and limit each other, even before there need be any talk of guilt and sin.

> This means that struggle is recognized to be a fundamental sociological principle; in principle it is hallowed. In concrete terms this acknowledges the necessity and rightness of party interests in every community relationship. It is only in the clash of wills that life springs forth; only in struggle does strength unfold.
>
> (D. Bonhoeffer)

If this were the final law of creaturely society, the fundamental (Catholic) law for amicable human relations would be the Hobbesian struggle of all against all. Thus Kant: "Man desires peace and unity, but Nature knows better; it knows what is good for his species. Nature desires strife." Nietzsche speaks in similar terms.

Christ's cross must also encompass these "hallowed party interests" if it is to give rise to an authentic catholicity in the world. But this means that the attitude Christ adopts in his suffering must have transcended every possible contradiction, all possible clashes, every particular claim to be in the right. It is not enough for him to utter a commandment of reconciliation (anyone could do that): he must create a context in which every particular standpoint with its unqualified, particular right (and wrong) is embedded right from the outset in the all-embracing Catholic reality. This "dividing wall", too, is to be "thrown down".

Take note: the "hallowed" particularity and opposition of wills, arising from the creation, is not suspended in the Catholica. Thus Paul is right at the heart of disputes in his communities. But there is a Catholic way (on the basis of the cross) of reconciling these standpoints in "the peace of God which passes all understanding" (Phil 4:7). In his wrestling with the Corinthians, for instance, Paul works toward reconciliation with all his strength. Ultimately, however, all he can do is point and testify to the reconciliation that has already taken place in Christ's cross.

Why the cross? For God in his absolute wisdom there is nothing remarkable, so to speak, in transcending all particular and conflicting standpoints and ascertaining the share of the right that each has. But Jesus, as man, cannot play the part of the great sage, loftily superior to all standpoints. He must endure their clash; and the resulting suffering is itself the expression of the most active readiness on his part to step in, according to the

Father's will, on behalf of every individual. In this way he does not overcome the particular from outside, but, acknowledging what is relatively valid in it, leads it beyond itself from within.

Imitating the Inimitable

Initially it seems impossible to imitate Jesus. After all, he is the "only-begotten Son, in the bosom of the Father", the unique One who "comes from above", manifesting his sublime nature (shared by no other man) in his humiliation. That is why we often speak of "discipleship" (because he bids us follow him) rather than "imitation" (since it is impossible).

But Paul says, "Be imitators of me, as I am of Christ" (1 Cor 11:1), and the Letter of Peter urges us to follow in Jesus' footsteps since he has "left us an example". And the Johannine Lord says, with regard to the foot-washing, "An example have I given unto you". And finally, according to Luke, even discipleship is a matter of "taking up your cross daily", as Jesus bore his. Is this not bound to produce a tangle of misunderstandings?

Let us examine the most explicit text: "I rejoice in my sufferings for your sake, and in my flesh I complete what is lacking in Christ's afflictions for the sake of his body, that is, the church" (Col 1:24). To see what this "lacking" means we need to adduce two other, apparently contradictory, texts; only when taken together do they point us to the full truth. On the one hand we read, "I am crucified with Christ. . . . I bear on my body the marks of Jesus" (Gal 2:20; 6:17); and on the other hand: "Is Christ divided? Was Paul crucified for you?" (1 Cor 1:13).

Both passages point to the central mystery. The cross of Jesus suffices for all (i.e., it is "Catholic"), and in its fullness it has room for us to enter right inside it. It gives us God's grace not only as its end product, but as the event of grace that it is. It is not a complacent fullness but a fullness that creates space within it, not a mere flowing outward (*bonum diffusivum sui*) but a fullness that opens up its inner riches, becoming poor for our sake (2 Cor 8:9) in order to make us rich, so that we may become "poor in spirit" with him and in him.

At this point we must remember that the figure of Jesus can be read properly only in a trinitarian context. He who, in John 11, calls himself "the Resurrection and the life" twice prays to the Father in the same chapter, in the context of the raising of Lazarus. He receives the power to work miracles from the Father (just as he receives from the Father the power of "having life in himself"—Jn 5:26); ultimately he is himself, the only begotten Son of God, on the basis of his perfect surrender to the Father. Receiving himself as gift, he surrenders himself; and because he surrenders himself, he receives himself. Moreover, the surrender to the Father that results in the Son having life in himself is a surrender to a Father who has always given himself to the Son. Otherwise he could not be the Father, the source of divine fullness. Right from the start, therefore, in its very wellsprings, the divine fullness is one that creates room, makes itself poor; by its poverty it enriches the Son with the Father's own godhead.

Here the catholicity of the godhead, of which we have already spoken, clearly becomes the origin of the catholicity of the Church, which is given a share in the act of redemption on the cross without in the least calling into question the uniqueness, the inimitable and sufficient nature of the Son's cross. The two aspects are simultaneous, expressing the two related images of the Church as "body" and "bride" of Christ: "body" in that the Church is made into a vessel, an organ, an extension of Christ through his self-communication, and "bride" or "spouse" in that it is fashioned by the Bridegroom's self-surrender and thus presented by him to himself (Eph 1:23; 5:25–27). This "partner" owes its existence to him who is the "origin"; he brings it into his own, original sphere and endows it with his qualities.

Immediacy Mediated

On the cross, through the bearing of sins and the overcoming of all resistance, an area of compassion is disclosed. Disclosed, too, are the Father, who gives himself to the Son, and the Son, who gives himself to the Father by actively surrendering himself: both are disclosed in a single act which is the Holy Spirit common to both. It is he, the Spirit of the mutual "poverty" of Father and Son, who draws men into the divine fullness of both that is prodigally squandered on the world.

The Son's eucharistic self-giving, too, with the Father's permission (indeed, as a fulfillment of the *berakah*, it owes its existence to the Father), is not the act of a mighty ruler "annexing" the Church to himself by his own power. It is the Spirit, "breathed forth" from the Father and from the crucified and risen Son after his return to the Father, the Spirit who is now the product and active result of their mutual love for the world, who penetrates this world. He does so in such a way as to endow it with the freedom and spontaneity to let itself be assimilated into the offered fullness. The "We" of Father and Son, meeting man's "I", can teach him to say "we" at such a deep level that now, "participating in the divine nature", he senses that all his particular freedoms and "personal" views and standpoints are undergirded by his membership of a whole, a whole that transforms his particularities into ministries.

Thomas Aquinas continually stresses that the members and parts love the body, the whole, more than themselves. This can be true at the organic level and also at the level of a sociology that regards the individual as a "part" of a political whole. But what happens if these individuals become persons who each stand in an "immediate" relation to God, in the "image and likeness" of the divine freedom? The ancient world's metaphor no longer applies, as we can see from the sociological situation of the modern world, which, post-Christian as it is, still has a tincture of the Christian idea of freedom. For it vacillates between the emancipation of the micro-ego in anarchic sovereignty and the emancipation of a "we", a macro-ego, in a collective tyranny that absorbs the freedom of the individual; both claim universality, but what they portray is only a personal *apartheid* or a collective *party*.

At precisely this point, in the face of these distorted models, the question arises as to the shape of a really Catholic "we", called into being by God's Holy Spirit. Such a "we" draws its life from the communicated fullness of Christ and the Father. This communication does not mean that the individual is presented with something alien to which, as a slave, he must dedicate his personal freedoms; rather, he is liberated from the restrictions of sin, but also from the particularism that is rooted in creation. As a result, and in a way that exceeds all hope, each of his freedoms finds itself in a broad space where, released from all narrowness, it can make its personal contribution to the whole on the basis of the equally personal Spirit of the Whole. At this point we begin to discern the features of the Church.

Church: Mission and Structure

Wave–Particle

According to the Good News, God in Christ has reconciled the world to himself. In Christian teaching it is a heresy to say that God has only chosen certain people for this reconciliation and has looked in mercy effectively on them alone. It is never even faintly suggested that God has redeemed (only) the Church. God's Catholic work is not sectarian but Catholic in design and scope. "God so loved the *world* that he gave his only Son" (emphasis added).

But John 3:16 goes on, "that whoever believes in him should not perish but have eternal life". But "how are they to believe in him of whom they have never heard?" (Rom 10:14). If the reconciliation of the world was to take place through a historically datable event, it was necessary to arrange for news of it to be spread "in Jerusalem and in all Judea and Samaria and to the end of the earth" (Acts 1:8).

This is something dynamic, like a source of light sending a pure beam into the darkest corner. Jesus has died and has returned to the Father; true, his Spirit is there, but will he be able to imprint himself on the recalcitrant matter of history without an instrument capable of shaping that same history? Jesus himself chose people and sent them out, tentatively at first, only to the lost sheep of the House of Israel, and then finally and definitively to all nations to the end of time.

There is a temptation to define these people, or the Church they constitute, in terms of pure mission: they are to radiate Christ into the world. There is a temptation to forbid them to reflect on their own nature and to see such reflection as a turning-aside from their commission, as an interruption of the clear stream they are meant to be. They are supposed to want to be nothing more than the "hyphen" that traverses world history, linking Christ with the Kingdom of God that is expected at the end of time.

The question arises, however, how there can be mission without a missionary, a sending-out without someone sent. Christ himself was pure mission from the Father, but he had to know who he was in order to be able to point away from himself and toward the Father. In this sense a purely functional christology is a contradiction that in no way does justice to Holy Scripture unless, at least implicitly, it is also structural and ontological. The question "Who are you?" echoes through all the Gospels, and Jesus responds to it by avoiding the traps it contains, which once again shows that he knows his personal identity. It is an identity, of course, that is co-extensive with his mission.

The same question "Who are you?" is continually and of necessity being addressed to Christ's ambassadors, and they cannot take refuge in some anonymous "radiation", leaving the answer to Christ and the Holy Spirit. The witnesses must produce their papers; they themselves must be able to substantiate their faith and their mission. And if they present the New Testament as their documentary evidence and use it to demonstrate not only their faith but also their personal commission, they thereby show that their letters of accreditation belong, not just to anyone, but to them.

Of course, this reveals the whole paradox of the Catholic Church. It is the pure radiation of Christ into the world, and, in order to radiate, it must also be a structure. It is both in motion "away from itself" and abiding "in itself". It is both wave and particle, dynamic and static. It is not like an association that is registered as an entity and pursues aims "for the benefit of members". The reconciliation of the world has already been achieved, and Christ's selection of the individual messengers ("he called to him those whom he wished") is simultaneous with this work of reconciliation: as the Light of the World (Jn 8:12), he has already appointed his chosen messengers to be the "light of the world" (Mt 5:14). The Church *is* first and foremost the radiation of the redemption (far beyond all structure), and in order to be this radiation it *has* structure.

The Church is one element within Jesus Christ's work of reconciliation. Consequently it shares—in appropriate measure—in the insoluble paradoxes that surround him, i.e., that it is precisely in his humiliation that Jesus shows his greatness, and that it is by pointing exclusively to the Father that he gives expression to his own unique personality.

In its paradoxical unities the Church, which is composed of sinners and fallible human beings, and which, for two thousand years, has offered an unprotected flank to the world, is much easier to dismantle. But the fact that she is constantly accused of contradictory traits points back to the christological paradox.

The Church, it is said, is too ascetic and takes too much delight in the world; she is too severe (celibacy, the indissolubility of marriage) and too lax; she is too dependent on the Old Testament ("holiness through works") and too "antisemitic"; she is the snivelling failures' religion of suffering (Nietzsche), but blesses secular weapons or uses them herself, against outside opponents (the Crusades) or enemies within (the Inquisition). Protestants accuse her of being too concerned with tradition; Orthodox, of being too little concerned.

The Church's sacramental practice is too close to folklore, or else it is too remote from everyday reality. She is too interior and world-denying, so say those whose commitment is political, while others complain that she is too activist, too conformist, too compromised by the capitalist half of the world. She clings to her schools and hospitals (the beginning and end of life), but her interest in the efforts of mature humanity is small or marked by distrust (e.g., the fate of Teilhard). She is much too tolerant, running after every modernity, ever since she incorporated Platonism and subsequently Aristotelianism into herself, right up to the present day when she is getting tangled up with the Jewish philosophy of hope—and at the same time she is the epitome of intolerance.

The litany is endless. Seeing the Church from the front, the critic complains that he cannot see the back; the critic who stands behind her feels insulted that she does not turn round to him. More precisely, what the one sees as her "grandeur", another regards as her "misère". Provided this "misère" reflects the "misère" of Christ (and is not simply the self-incurred misery of sin), both "grandeur" and "misère" could be grasped as identical, and this would provide a basis for discipleship in both cases. True, in the realm of phenomena the Church's disparate aspects can be added together and totalled, but her catholicity is like that of her Lord, whom she reflects: she transcends quantity, however great and comprehensive. She cannot adequately be defined because she is part of the mystery of God; participating in this mystery is of her very essence.

Is Too Much Demanded of the Christian?

But is it possible for the Christian (let alone the outsider) to get any picture at all of the *Catholica*? Does it not look like the image produced by a series of film negatives, one on top of the other? If there were fewer there would be a clearer picture! From all sides he hears, "Nowadays the Church ought to . . ." And what ought she to do? The most diverse and contrary things. And what is the Christian supposed to do? And then, when he sees finite human beings (bishops, for example) trying to please everyone, it makes him positively sick and he feels like getting out. After all, Christ was no trapeze-artist.

(Is that so certain? One would almost like to query it. Think of Rilke's Saltimbanques. However:) Given that he was not, surely he *did* succeed, amazingly, and from some inaccessible vantage point, in reconciling opposites? Might it not be that the Church is empowered and required to do something similar? Furthermore, is not the Church the one Body with many members, all of which, according to Paul, in their diverse and opposing functions, are permeated by the one Spirit?

Let the despairing and vexed man ask himself what is his personal mission, n.b., within the *whole*. It has a clear profile and is ideally suited to him, but only insofar as it is part of a Body with an all-embracing mission. He need have anxiety neither as regards the clear circumscribing of his mission (for this will not cause him to drop out of the divine infinitude) nor as regards the integration of his mission in a total picture that comprehends and requires other, perhaps opposed, tasks; the two are inseparably one. The most famous example of this is the "little way" of Thérèse of Lisieux, on the basis of which she is called "Patroness of the Missions" for the entire organism of the Church. Everyone who performs his own task in a Catholic spirit is contributing to the Church's catholicity.

"You Are the Light of the World"

The mission of the messengers of faith is to radiate to all the world the light of God's reconciliation in Christ. It is not enough for them merely to tell about this light. Their conviction and their words themselves must have a light-quality about them; they must *be* this radiance. Their light is a light that has been given to them, a "borrowed light". (The Church has often been compared to the moon, receiving her light from Christ, her Sun.) All the same, it is not a spurious light, not a mere "reflection" (K. Barth), but a true and actual light.

This means that the Church has been given two gifts that characterize her very core, though they are not coterminous in every respect. First she has been given the authority, the power, to speak and act in the name of Jesus. "And he appointed twelve, to be with him, and to be sent out to preach and have authority to cast out demons" (Mk 3:14f.). "He who hears you hears me" (Lk 10:16). The messengers are so empowered to speak and act in matters of salvation that the authority of him who sends them is present in them. Their mission is holy as such: he who sends them guarantees his divine presence in them.

The other gift is personal to the messenger: he is made a *light*. If his mission lives in him and he in his mission, he will catch fire. But it is not his own fire, his enthusiasm, that he wants to spread, but the fire of his Lord. He does not confuse himself with his Lord. If he knows his place there is no danger of a confusion here; God will see to it.

It can happen that an individual possesses the objective holiness of mission and authority and yet has no subjective holiness. This is a grave misfortune, dangerously obscuring the Church's mission. But the Church as a whole can never fail to possess both gifts at the same time. This equally applies to the Church in its visible aspect. Consequently it will not do to divide the Catholic Church into two churches: an empirical Church with her authority and her ascertainable membership, and an invisible Church of saints, whose number is known only to God. Augustine saw very clearly that the visible bearer of the power of the keys cannot receive a sinner back into the

Communio Sanctorum without the forgiveness (together with God) of the Church of the saints, which the Song of Songs calls the "one dove". But he does not draw the same conclusion as that Augustinian friar, Luther, namely, that only the Church of the saints with its "priesthood of all believers" has the true power of the keys. In Augustine the tension persists: Christ's Church has objective and subjective holiness, but they coincide perfectly only in Christ, the Church's head.

"I Am With You Always"

The Son of God did not wish to come into the world without his Mother's *Fiat*; similarly he wanted to spend his public life in the company of the Twelve. Thus, on the night before he suffered, he gave them his flesh and blood, so that the sacrifice of Golgotha might be in them, even in the hour of darkness when the Shepherd would be struck down and the flock scattered. The Twelve share a common life in which he is their "superior", their "Lord and Master" (Jn 13:13). By doing so, from his side, he has definitively entered into the community of those he sends out in his name, even if it is only after his Resurrection that they can really receive him with living faith, hold fast to him and be sent out by him.

He puts himself unreservedly and without qualification into the community of the Twelve, making over to them his own catholicity, even the "Kingdom" the Father has given to him (Lk 22:29). In the future he will live in his Church, which is both mission and institution; its static aspect is only there so that it may dynamically transcend itself in the direction of the ultimate "Kingdom" (1 Cor 15:24). Henceforth it is only with and in his Church, which Paul calls his "body", that he will be present and available to the world—the ever-growing Kingdom. The reiterated "all" at the end of Saint Matthew's Gospel shows that Christ's catholicity is opened up, in the catholicity of his Church, to a future catholicity of the world: "*All* authority in Heaven and on earth has been given to me. Go therefore and make disciples of *all* nations, baptizing them in the name of the Father and of the Son and of the Holy Spirit, teaching them to observe *all* that I have commanded you; and, lo, I am with you *always*, to the close of the age" (Mt 28:19–20, emphasis added).

"The Arrow of Longing"

The earthly mission of Jesus was consummated in his return to the Father. His mission in world history and in the Church will be consummated when he places the perfected Kingdom at his Father's feet, so that God may be all in all. The

Church journeys toward this absolute and unsurpassable catholicity; her mission does not stop at an immanent transformation of the world, she wrenches the world beyond her immanence and "immanent transcendence" and points her to her final goal, creation's raison d'être. Everything about the Church is in motion toward this destination.

The impatience of Jesus—"I came to cast fire on the earth; and would that it were already kindled!"—is also the Church's constant impatience: "The Spirit and the Bride say, 'Come.'" But there is also the patience of Jesus, not preempting the Father's hour; he urges the Church to exercise the same patience, albeit in vigilant wakefulness: "Let your loins be girded and your lamps burning" What seems to be an endless standing still is in God's sight the highest speed, namely, expectancy and readiness for him.

Everything that seems to be static in the Church is only either the trigger of her dynamism or some residue of this dynamism. Scripture is there only to enable the Word to go about "unfettered" (2 Tim 2:9) in its pristine freshness. The sacraments are there only to ensure that the act of redemption—the cross, Resurrection, and Pentecost—remains ever-present and never sinks to the level of a mere memory. Authority is there lest the Christian content himself with mediocre ideals; it ensures that he stands under the norm of his living

Lord. Dogma is there only to prevent faith veering to right or to left of the *mysterium*, to keep it docile to the Lord's fashioning of life and faith.

> The static element in the Church is not its own raison d'être. It could be shown to be only apparently static, for in reality it is a precipitate, something condensed out of the dynamic element, like a ray of light which must be split by a prism so that human understanding may grasp it. Dogma, however, cannot be explained on the basis of such elements, for it always transcends and thus transforms them. If dogma is the perfect norm of all spiritual life, it is only because the authentic spiritual life is nothing other than dogma *in actu*.
>
> (Henri de Lubac)

Down through the centuries the Church's longing may seem to have embraced many a secular element, enlivening it, kindling it and ultimately leaving it behind as a charred relic. But this is only true of peripheral forms and formulae. Where she sees forms and formulae that express the very essence of her mission, however, she never lets go of them. She keeps them safe in her supra-historical, eschatological core, however much, from the merely historical standpoint, they may seem to be the inert ballast of tradition. This is true of decisive conciliar definitions (Nicaea, Chalcedon, etc.); their continued vitality cannot be explained in purely historical terms. They are not merely baggage carried on the journey: they actively journey along with us.

Retrospect as Prospect

Our whole preoccupation with the origins of Christianity, with the pre-Easter life of Jesus, with the as yet rudimentary faith of the disciples, would be nothing but unfruitful "archaeology" (Fernand Guimet) if we were to settle down in that era, confusing the beginnings with the consummation, and to try to exist "at the same time" as the historical Jesus. It makes sense for a person to attempt to do this only if he regards Christ as absent from the Church's present. Jesus rebuked the disciples for their lack of faith and constantly directed their thoughts to the coming consummation. Paul no longer wants to know Christ "after the flesh".

Jesus himself was perfect in every phase of his earthly path. For authentic faith, therefore, to look back to him is always to look forward to the perfection that, by way of anticipation, has seized me in all my imperfection. "I press on to make it my own, because Christ Jesus has made me his own" (Phil 3:12f.).

The Alpha already contains the Omega; the Alpha has a propelling effect and comes to meet us, from the future, in the form of the Omega.

And as for each here-and-now encounter (in word, in sacrament, in the interpersonal situation, in prayer), it is not a standing still; it actually stimulates and accelerates this propulsion and attraction.

Travelling Light

> A bird is active, because a bird is soft. A stone is helpless, because a stone is hard. The stone must by its own nature go downwards, because hardness is weakness. The bird can of its nature go upwards, because fragility is force. In perfect force there is a kind of frivolity, an airiness that can maintain itself in the air. . . . Angels can fly because they can take themselves lightly. This has been always the instinct of Christendom. . . . Pride is the downward drag of all things into an easy solemnity. One "settles down" into a sort of selfish seriousness; but one has to rise to a gay self-forgetfulness. . . . It is much easier to write a good *Times* leading article than a good joke in *Punch*. For solemnity flows out of men naturally; but laughter is a leap. It is easy to be heavy: hard to be light. Satan fell by the force of gravity.
>
> (Chesterton, *Orthodoxy*)

Kierkegaard, who constantly uses the word "serious", looks wistfully over the hedge to the Catholic world where, as he puts it, the Christian always senses a certain "rascality". Should the Catholic show this Protestant (who was so angry with Luther for having jettisoned "works"—the ascetical and religious life) how to cast one's burden on the Lord and (*sola fide!*) rest in his arms? Should we say that complete seriousness is found only in God? True enough, if we look at the cross, which delivers us from our sinful seriousness. But even the terrible gravity of the cross is a product of the perfect poise of divine love; and this love, so to speak, has a reckless courage: thus the Father has the courage to let his Son fall into hell's abyss; the Son, sinking into the bottomless depths, has the courage to commend himself into the Father's hands (which he cannot feel); and the Spirit boldly acts as the pure, mutual essence of this reckless courage.

On the Other Hand

Ignatius bids us reflect on how "God toils in all things". We should consider what a burden this universe, with all its competing freedoms, is to God, who wants to bring them "whither they do not wish to go", yet without his grace overpowering them in an external manner. We should come to understand that the "unutterable groanings" of the Spirit come from the very depths of our hearts, but also from the "agony of Jesus to the end of the world", and also from the Woman of the Apocalypse who cries out in giving birth, not only to the Messiah, but also to all those who come after, who "bear testimony to Jesus" (Rev 12:17). Ignatius goes on to observe that the Church (for who else could the Woman be?) will always share in this toil; there will always be those ready to help bear the burden that the world imposes on God, his Son and his Church. They think of themselves least of all; they so forget themselves that they take on immoderate and senseless penances, simply in order somehow to reduce by a little the immense weight. Paul, too, chastises his body, and not by "beating the air"; nor does he dispense himself from this practice on the grounds of the countless sufferings heaped on him externally. In the heart of the Church there is the small company whose members cannot look at the sufferings of the crucified God without humbly asking not to be totally excluded from them.

Institution as Discipline

It is only because the Church's internal structure has authority and an official dimension that she can admonish and encourage the imperfect Christian to pursue his own special mission. Of course it is important for the "official" side of the Church to react with understanding to the distress, difficulties and helplessness of Christians, but it is even more important that the Christian should continually aspire to the authoritatively presented norm that is mediated and rendered concrete in everyday life by manifold Church practices. (Nowadays the tendency is to loosen, abolish or spiritualize a large part of these mediatory practices. The question is: Does this not cause the gospel norm to become abstract, remote from daily life, and ultimately forgotten?)

In this respect, the "institution" is a "necessary evil" (but could this not be said of Christ's cross too?), since human nature, crawling on the ground, needs to be held up by a trellis if it is to bear fruit. At baptism the Christian promises, not a half faith, but a full faith, involving discipleship. Who can help him to combat his own fragility and strive toward "what he would" but "cannot" do because of his own inauthenticity? The "institution" should be nothing other than a help, liberating the freedom of the Christian man so that it can find its true nature.

It is no small matter if a person sometimes does reluctantly what he should really do gladly (e.g., attending Mass every Sunday), for there is hope that eventually he may be moved to do it spontaneously, out of an inner desire. Everything put forward by the institution as a "must" is in fact a privilege. It is the privilege of sharing in an event of the greatest significance for the world, in collaboration with the Church, or rather, *as the Church*, in the form of a mission within her.

The official side of the Church, with her discipline, is an essential form of the presence of the cross, causing us to feel the hardness, the implacability, the hiddenness of the divine love. It is customary to trace the sacraments back to the blood and water that flowed from the Lord's opened side; they could not be administered at any less cost than this; but who, attending a celebration of the Eucharist, thinks of this "price" (1 Cor 6:20)? This is the context for the issue of sexual discipline in the Church, a practice by no means "time-bound" but which the Apostle deduces from the most profound dogmatic interrelationships in connection with the great "price" of salvation. Our bodies are members of Christ, "one flesh" with him through the Eucharist and through the indwelling of the divine Spirit in them. None of this is affected by the imposing or removing of taboos in the sexual area.

There is a final consideration, which is also primary: institution is given to us as a concrete symbol, showing us that we cannot grasp grace by our own power: we can only receive it. (Naturally this applies equally to the priest who administers word and sacrament; he is subject, in what he says and does, to the "given" nature of the institution.) We must drink at the source. These words are addressed to "sons", not "servants". We are privileged to pray whenever we wish, to open the Bible at will, to perform every work of charity at the Spirit's behest. We are free. But we are free *as members of Christ's Church*, which is his wedded Bride. Even the spontaneous union of man and woman has its immanent laws, in which "may" and "must" coincide in the act of love.

The Alternative

In the pagan era on the threshold of the Lord's advent, all social and political institutions had a religious quality: this represented a humanizing of the divine justice on a world scale. In the Old Testament the strict framework embodies the covenant-righteousness of Yahweh, which is also his grace and mercy, pointing forward to the coming fulfillment when the external law will be transposed into people's hearts. This takes place, as we have shown, in the Church.

This means that the pre-Christian order has been inwardly superseded; the post-Christian state will continue, for a time, to be supported by the religiosity and ethics of its Christian citizens. If their strength fails, the institution society needs lest it sink into anarchy will become iron-plating, leaving the individual no room to breathe as a person. It makes no difference to the enslaved person whether the institution is totalitarian at a national or international level. In regions such as this the institution of the Church, insofar as it still has any room to maneuver, becomes an island of freedom. Then many people can experience directly the fact that mission (radiation) and structure mutually condition each other within the Church; at the core, indeed, they are one.

An Atmosphere

As far as the essence and the inner form of the Church are concerned, no human word is proof against misunderstanding. "Body of Christ" and "Bride of Christ" are two images that partly conflict with and partly (as metaphors) supplement each other. The Church is the area where the fullness of God's grace in Christ is to be made available to the world, an area both permanent ("structure") and transient ("mission"); she is both the immediate presence of Christ (and of God in him), his extension (the Body/Head relationship) and his partner (the response to his word).

None of these relationships can be isolated from the others. Christ's saving work is immediately present, for instance, in the Eucharist: the priest does not stand in a mediating position between the believer and the Lord; rather, arising from his having received the fullness of consecration, he is the actualization and guarantee of this immediacy. Thus he is the very reverse of a diversion or detour. But if we regard the Church as Christ's partner, giving answer to his word, this distance is both created by the Holy Spirit, the divine "We", and immediately suspended by him; for the answer can only be an echo of his word; the answer's freedom and appropriateness is achieved by the Spirit of Christ, who liberates our freedom. ("For we do not know what to ask, but the Spirit intercedes for us.") The Spirit bears witness with our spirit that we (in, with and through Christ) are the sons of God; and when the cry of "Abba!" is heard, who utters it: Christ in us, or we ourselves, or the Spirit?

Everything is like this in the Church. From the outside she looks like an "establishment", like one organization among others. From within she is the medium—one might almost say, the magic— whereby God is able to be all in all within his creation, without suppressing the creature he has made free. In fact, by doing this, he perfects his creature at her own proper level, giving her a most intimate share in his incomparable nature.

The Communion of Saints

Luther

This is the communion of saints of which we
boast. . . . Is it not good for us to dwell here,
where all the members suffer when one suffers,
and, if one member is set forth in glory, all rejoice
with him? If I suffer, I do not suffer alone: Christ
and all Christians suffer with me, as the Lord says:
"Anyone who touches you touches the apple of
my eye." Thus others carry my burden, and their
strength is mine. The Church's faith comes to the
aid of my timidity, the chastity of others holds out
while my lustful nature is tempted, the fasting of
others brings advantage to me, another's prayers
intercede for me. Thus, in truth, I can boast in the
goods of others as in my own. And they really are
my own if I take delight in them. I may be disreputable and dirty, yet those I love and applaud
are beautiful and graceful. With this love I appropriate not only their goods, but themselves; and
so, in virtue of their honor, my disreputable self
attains repute; my lack is supplied from their super-
fluity; in virtue of their merits [eorum merita] my
sins are healed. Who, therefore, could despair of
his sins? Who would not rejoice in his punishments, since he himself does not bear his sins and
punishments? Or at least he does not bear them on

his own, for there are so many holy sons of God, and Christ himself, lending him aid.

Anyone who does not believe that this takes place is an infidel; he has abjured Christ and the Church. Even if a person does not feel it, it truly happens; and who is there, in the end, who does not feel it? When you do not despair, when you do not lose your patience, what is the cause of it? Your own virtue? Certainly not. It comes from the communion of saints. When we say that the Church is holy, what do we mean except that it forms the communion of saints? With whom, however, do the saints hold communion? With the good as with the wicked. For everything belongs to all, as the sacrament of the altar shows us visibly in bread and wine: here the Apostle calls us one body, one bread, and one drink. What another suffers, I suffer and endure; the good things he meets come to me too. Christ says the same: what is done to the least of his children is done to him. Receiving the least particle of the sacrament of the altar, we have assuredly received the whole loaf. And anyone who despises this tiniest particle has despised the loaf.

Let us think on these things, therefore, when we are suffering, when we are dying. Let us firmly believe, let us be convinced, that it is not we or we alone who suffer, but Christ and the Church suffer, endure and die together with us. Christ did not want our path of death, from which every man withdraws in fear, to be a lonely path; he appointed that we should be accompanied by the whole Church along the path of suffering and death. In fact, the Church suffers more than we do, and we can adopt the words Elisha [2 Kings 6] addressed to his faint-hearted servant: "Fear not, for those who are with us are more than those who are with them. Then Elisha prayed, and said, O Lord, I pray thee, open his eyes that he may see. So the Lord opened the eyes of the young man, and he saw; and behold, the mountain was full of horses and chariots of fire round about Elisha." So all we have to do is to pray for our eyes to be opened so that we can see, with the eyes of faith, the Church all around us; then we need fear nothing any more.

(Luther, *Tessaradecas*, 1520)

Communio in Its Catholic Meaning

What Catholic would not agree with this magnificent passage of Luther's? Basing himself on words of Paul, he is describing something dear to the heart of the Catholica, namely, the mysterious osmosis between the members of the "Body of Christ", which does not stop at the interchange of external goods but extends to a sharing in what is most personal. In French one can speak of a "réversibilité des mérites", and the word "merit" comes quite naturally to Luther, just as he is not afraid to speak of an unheard-of "work" when Moses desires to be rejected instead of the sinful people and when Paul wishes to be accursed and banished from Christ instead of his Jewish brothers: "The work is inaccessible to reason, for it is too high" (*Werke*, 10, III, 219). It is a pity that, with the years, this view of things (which comes wholly from the Catholic tradition) faded more and more into the background in Luther. "It did not survive in Lutheranism and did not become part of its doctrinal development" (P. Althaus). The horizontal aspect is pushed "far out of sight behind the sole supernatural bond linking the members with the Head" (E. Kohlmeyer).

The reasons for this are due, no doubt, to the loss of certain Catholic elements. Such loss is not evident in the passage quoted, but it arises from other central Reformation tenets and endangers the catholicity of the *Communio Sanctorum*. The two most important of these tenets are the separation of faith from works, and the separation of the invisible Church of the saints from the visible, official Church (or what remained of it in the Reformed churches). First of all, however, we must discuss what makes such a *Communio* possible.

Rooted in Christ

The very fact that the original meaning of the *Communio Sanctorum* is "communion in holy things", i.e., first and foremost in the Eucharist

—"the bread we break, is it not a communion in the body of Christ?" (1 Cor 10:16)—shows us that the members of the mystical Body do not exchange their so-called "merits" in an arbitrary way: their sharing of goods is based on the fact that they are all rooted in Christ. (Among Christians, at least, the external sharing of alms and other corporal works of mercy takes place in the Spirit of Christ and in thankful remembrance of him.)

The earth in which they are rooted is personal and supernatural, i.e., it has nothing in common with C. G. Jung's "collective unconscious". It is personal: each member-person is called upon to open himself to the shared stream created in the entire organism by the circulation of goods, like the blood's circulation in the human body. (This is a first and most significant aspect of devotion to the Sacred Heart.)

This explains something that at first seems very strange, namely, that only in Christianity does the good prove fruitful above and beyond the individual. On the basis of the physiological model one would be inclined to think that the infection of one member would lead to a general blood-poisoning. But, while the Apostle speaks of evil spreading by infection, there is no question of evil bearing fruit. The view of Origen and Tyconius, that there is a mystical body of the devil as the negative counterpart to the Body of Christ, is unbiblical and theologically contradictory.

The idea of representative action or suffering on

someone's behalf, as Bonhoeffer rightly says, rests on an offer on God's part and therefore "applies only in Christ and his community. It is not an ethical possibility: it is a theological concept." He goes on to say that, while there may be "an ethical concept of representation", that is, "the freewill acceptance of an evil on behalf of someone else", such action neither "penetrates to the other person's responsibility for himself" nor does the latter "commit his whole ethical person, but only as much as he owes to the agent who has acted on his behalf". In the "communion of the saints" these bounds are overstepped and people's intimate personal areas are affected: this is only possible in and through Christ. The "merit", therefore, is exclusively at Christ's service, although, in handing it over, the Christian may link it with some quite specific request or intention. Everything passes through Christ's and God's freedom, and this prevents any direct experience —let alone calculation—of cause and effect. Such experience may be given from time to time, in an inchoate form, as a brief lifting of a curtain that is normally closed.

Loneliness and the "Communion of Saints"

Jesus, who "was made to be sin for us", "died in loneliness, and so the disciples too, in a present that had no future, had to be lonely too". To us, who have been given Easter as well as Good Friday, the death of Jesus is retrospectively illuminated by "the light of victory". "This results in the paradoxical reality of a community of the cross that represents innermost loneliness and innermost communion at the same time. And this communion is the specifically Christian communion" (Bonhoeffer). The loneliness of the cross, archetypally and once for all in the death of Jesus, gives birth to community, which will continue to be created anew in the grace of the Church.

There are moments when a solitary Christian undergoes suffering that is unknown to others or not understood by them; he offers it to the Lord for him to use as he thinks fit, and so this Christian becomes a source of new community. In the Church's history there have also been times "when the Church existed only in a single person or a family" (Augustine), when her catholicity withdrew back into her root: consider the loneliness of an Athanasius or a Maximus Confessor. Consider, too, the loneliness of a few monks still embodying the authentic tradition of their founder. This is a loneliness without earthly hope; the crucified Lord, too, had no earthly hope, yet "against all hope" he is able to raise up children to Abraham from the very stones.

Faith is a movement of the entire person away from himself, through the gift of grace; thereby he lays hold of the mercy of God given to him in Christ—in the form of the forgiveness of sins, justification and sanctification. In this movement away from himself man has done all that he, through grace, can do; he has done all that God requires of him. Since his intention is to leave himself, without reservation, and hand himself over entirely, this movement implicitly contains all the "works" he will eventually do. They are not some second entity beside faith; if they are performed in a Christian spirit, they are only forms in which faith expresses itself.

As an act of the whole person, faith travels in a direction away from itself and toward God. That is why reflection on itself and any attempt to make itself secure are foreign to it. The gospel may promise a "reward in Heaven" to a faith that is rightly lived out, but faith itself is very far from calculating any "merit" that may bring about such a reward.

The word "merit", insofar as it concerns some value conferring a right to something, is theologically an unhappy term that would be better dropped. (In tradition it very often has a quite different sense, namely, "being found worthy" by God: *tu quae meruisti portare* . . .) We need have no qualms about dropping the word, for there is a biblical word ready to replace it: fruitfulness. God responds to Abraham's faith in this way: "I will make you exceedingly fruitful; and I will make nations of you" (Gen 17:6). The Lord is always using the word in his parables. In John it is the grain of wheat, which dies in the earth, that brings forth much fruit. The metaphor of the vine is even clearer. Apart from Jesus a man can do "nothing", but if he abides in him he brings forth "much" fruit. If he fails to do this, he is removed; if he succeeds, he is "cleansed", cut back in order to produce "even more fruit".

Clearly, this does not mean externally quantifiable results. As far as the Kingdom of God is concerned, Mary, sitting at the feet of Jesus, is more fruitful than the busy Martha. When Mary anoints the Lord's feet at the meal in Bethany and Judas protests at this "waste" and thinks how much money the ointment would have yielded, he is rebuked: the fruitfulness of this prodigal gesture that takes no account of "merit" is far more important to Jesus than some work of charity.

Living in Fruitfulness

This is the origin of many forms of life and devotion in the Catholica which have caused offense to those looking on from outside. Indeed, they will not be made any less offensive if we replace "meritorious" with "fruitful". The latter is a metaphor too, of course, for the human being is not a fruit tree; but mothers and poets are also referred to as fruitful, and it is not difficult to see the meaning behind the metaphor: here it means being of service for God's plans, which are always Catholic, all-embracing and for the good of mankind. Or, to take up the image of light that Jesus applies to himself and his disciples: a more complete surrender in faith can shed light over a wider area; it can radiate light into other hearts without them knowing where this light comes from.

Everything that has been developed down through the Church's history in the way of "contemplative" forms of life has always aimed at finding a manner of life that would sustain the fundamental act of surrender-in-faith, the pure answer to the word, as clearly and constantly as possible. This is what was intended at the Catholic core, whatever superficial misunderstandings there may have been. As we have already said, it was and is based on the conviction that this act of dedication to God contains its "work", its fruitfulness, within it, whereas the form of life that starts with external works (like Martha's) cannot be sure of being constantly motivated by the act of surrender-in-faith. What from the outside seems to be inactivity is from the inside of far greater effect than anything else—particularly if the believer's offer to God is used to incorporate himself into the passion of Jesus for the sake of the world.

It is on the basis of the radiating influence of Catholic life that a linguistically vulnerable term such as "works of supererogation" must be understood. The term comes from a background of Christian mediocrity that, however inappropriate, unfortunately does exist. Where God is concerned we should always give our utmost, everything that the creature can offer in response to God's all: the Catholic in return for the Catholic. The mediocre Christian allots himself a measure that seems appropriate to him and considers anyone who gives more to be a professional saint. It is important to realize that the genuine saint never sees his offer to God as something beyond the norm, as a work beyond what is required. We shall return to this issue shortly.

The radiant light of love that shines from the cross is joined by a light from the Church, which does not want its Yes to be limited in any way. This radiance is inwardly inexhaustible (for it is not dependent on a finite mass of combustible material). Consequently the idea of the Church's "treasury" arises quite naturally. It is foolish to say that this image, which Jesus himself uses ("Give everything away, and you will have treasure in Heaven") is impersonal and overly material. The Prodigal Son, returning home to confess his sinful path and encountering more fatherly love than he had dared to hope for, experienced the existence of this treasure. Since Jesus intervenes on behalf of the world together with all those who try, with him, to be a "light", who try to utter and live out the Yes of complete surrender-in-faith— "Here am I, and the children God has given me" (Heb 2:13)—this wellspring and sanctuary of all fruitful, never-failing love can be called the Church's "treasury".

Furthermore, if Augustine's theory is right, namely, that Christ pardons the sinner together with the communion of saints, the communion of love, and that this pardon is administered, together with him, by the Church, which is officially empowered to do so, even the most extreme and most blatant abuse of such administration becomes to a degree understandable. Of course, every individual believer, since he is a child of God, has direct access to God and his mercy. But just as the Father, in forgiving him, does not forgive him over the heads of Christ and his Church, so too the believer is not meant to reach up for the overflowing divine love in isolation from Christ and the Church, which are the concrete forms of God's mercy. The Christian does not take things for himself: he is given them as gifts. So it is in the Eucharist: we do not go to the tabernacle and take a host for ourselves; so too when grave sin is to be absolved, the absolution is pronounced by the Church. And since, even when absolved from sin, a person has to "expiate the punishment due to sin", i.e., to undergo an existential path of purification, the Church—both the Church of the saints and the official Church—interceding for further grace, can assure him of a gentler path through purification and the Last Judgment. This is what is meant by "indulgence".

According to Paul, we must all undergo the fiery judgment of God (1 Cor 3:12–15). It will test each person's life's work, with quite different results: what some have built will stand, what others have built will burn away to nothing. In the Catholic milieu this personal "dimension" or "intensity" or "duration" of the process of judgment (which cannot be expressed in terms of time) is called "purgatory" or "place of purification" (or better: "purification process"). Nothing more than this is meant by the term. However personal and lonely this face-to-face encounter on man's part with his Judge may be (Rom 14:6, passim), the Judge is never separated from his Church. The Church accompanies the individual in his loneliest hour, even if he is unaware of it.

The Catholicity of the Individual Christian

It would not be enough to define the catholicity of the individual Christian in terms of his sharing in all the spiritual goods of the Catholica. This would be to see it, at most, as something passive and potential, and it would not tell us how much of these goods the limited individual can take into himself, or how much of them he can share with others. In other words, even if a man were fully justified through God's grace in Christ, this would still not tell us how far he was also sanctified, to what extent he had overcome his resistance to the Holy Spirit, who had been given him.

God's graces are Catholic, that is, all-embracing. They are not conditional or limited. But can anyone take the proffered grace into himself in a Catholic, all-embracing way, without conditions or limitations? The act of doing this would be nothing other than perfect faith, as we have already described it: namely, as the placing of one's whole life at God's disposal, as a Yes without limits. Unquestionably, we can describe such an act, if it exists anywhere, as perfect holiness, for such a creature would be totally open to the Holy Spirit.

In Catholic belief, this act must really exist if it is true that Christ wanted to "present the Church to himself in splendor, without spot or wrinkle or any such thing, that she might be holy and without blemish" (Eph 5:27). It is not enough that he alone should act on the Church's behalf and justify it, uttering the perfect Yes; the Church herself must speak her sanctifying and equally perfect "Amen —may it be so to me" (2 Cor 1:20ff.).

Furthermore, in Catholic belief this "Amen"

—through grace the unlimited Yes of faith—must resound at the very point at which the Word becomes flesh, so that the Yes becomes flesh in the person who puts no obstacle in the way; in this one on whom the Child Jesus will be dependent, and from whom he will learn how to utter faith's perfect Yes to God. If this Yes had never been uttered on earth, in fulfillment of the faith of Israel, the step from the synagogue (which was always defective) to the *ecclesia immaculata* (Eph 5:27) would never have been taken. The "Body" would have been fundamentally and eternally incommensurate with the "Head".

However, faith's Yes, its limitless readiness for all that God may desire and require, means that, in the context of the grace that empowers it (cf. Lk 1:28), the finite creature can really be "co-extensive" with God's catholicity. Not in what it does, but in what it allows to be done. The inner dimensions of this "allowing" reflect the *magis*-principle: "always more". If God increases his demands, if the path becomes steeper and harder (until it reaches the foot of the cross), the original Yes expands. Right from the start it had this elasticity. Origen calls such a soul "*anima ecclesiastica*": a soul with the dimensions of the Catholic Church. If it really has these dimensions, it is also the realized Catholica; it has the qualities of the "Body", enabling the Head to pour its fullness into it without encountering any resistance.

Others come close to this limitless Yes—always through grace—and so they are joined to and incorporated in the existing *ecclesia immaculata*. As individuals they also participate subjectively, according to their degree of readiness, in the quality of catholicity. As Möhler says, they are "Catholic" in the sense that they are integral parts of a Whole; or, as Peter Damian puts it more fully:

> [in its members] Christ's Church is intertwined with such love that it can be One in many; it can be the Whole, mysteriously, in countless numbers. And this comes about in such a way that the whole Church can rightly be designated by the single number, as the one Bride of Christ, and each individual soul—according to the same mystery—can be regarded as the whole Church.

So it is not simply a case of "where two or three are gathered together . . .", but also "where there is one . . .", provided that this one member is at pains inwardly to fill out the dimensions of the Catholic Yes. In concrete terms, the latter always contains Church and community and hence the presence of Christ.

The Spirit and the Yes That Creates the Church

The dialogue between the angel and Mary seems to be a purely private one, carried on in the "chamber" referred to in the Sermon on the Mount. But in

this dialogue, as in every perfect prayer, two dimensions open up: God's all-in-all and man's complete readiness. And the Holy Spirit descends from
the first to the second, bearing God's seed, the
seed of the Word, to implant it in the earthly
womb. From the beginning, however, this Spirit
is the divine "We": he is Person and community.
When Mary is greeted, right from the outset, as "full
of grace", this Spirit is already in her, fashioning
the Yes in her soul. Thus, whether she is aware of
it or not, the community, the Catholica, is already
present in her Yes; the whole faith of her nation is
ultimately formulated in it. Indeed, it recapitulates
whatever moment of dedication and readiness anyone ever had: according to Thomas Aquinas, Mary
responds "on behalf of the entire human race".
Therefore her Yes is open to the future as well,
sustaining all the attempts to say Yes that will be
made in the coming Church. The Church is already
there, in perfection, in her, because the Spirit in
whom she says Yes is always God's "We", who
has begun on earth his work of enabling us both to
say "We" and to be "We".

Sanctorum Communio in the Early Church

There is another dimension lacking, however, in
the splendid passage from Luther we have quoted;
it needs to be supplied if we are to appreciate the
whole scope of the Catholic understanding of

Communio. The deficiency is connected with the Protestant gulf between the (invisible) Church of saints and the (visible, empirical) imperfect Church provided with official ministries. These two aspects, however, have been inseparable from one another right from early Christian days. The *Communio* is based on both the sacramental dimension (preeminently in the Eucharist) and the juridical dimension, i.e., the bishop's plenitude of authority in guiding the community and representing it in its external relations. Only the person who celebrates Eucharist with him, who acknowledges the *Communio* that exists between community and bishop, belongs to the Catholica. Local churches are in *Communio* with one another, whether it is church writing to church (Letter of Clement, first century), bishop writing to church (Ignatius, beginning of second century), or bishop writing to bishop. But later the bishops can break off *Communio* between their church (diocese) and another if the latter's bishop comes under suspicion of heresy. This loosing of the bonds is called excommunication, the breaking-off of relations. For a long time no one asked who, ultimately, had the power to excommunicate. Suspicion was rife in the confused period of Arianism; there were puzzling situations in which two bishops communicated with a third and yet had suspended relations between themselves. Where are the criteria for authentic *Communio*? People appeal to the view of a majority of local churches, or to the opinion of the oldest communities, those founded by Apostles. But such criteria cannot be decisive. Ultimately the only way out was to appeal to the Bishop of Rome; but in any case he had held the "primacy of love" long before these perplexing cases arose (so Ignatius; here "agape" *can* be another term for *Communio*, as occurs frequently). "Because of its very special preeminence, all other churches are bound to agree with it", says Irenaeus as early as the second century. Here *"convenire"* ("agree") *can* be a translation of *koinonein* ("to hold *Communio*"). From ancient times Rome documented member churches and the norms of the *Communio* long before external circumstances made it imperative to find a juridical benchmark for its unity.[1]

We have anticipated here something that will be touched on in the next chapter; otherwise it would have been impossible to speak in a fully Catholic way of the "communion of saints". Christ was a visible, historical human being, and the Twelve were precisely ascertainable, historical personalities, entrusted with the task of leading the post-Easter Church. Accordingly, in succession to the Apostles and in constant reference to the successor of Peter, the communion of saints remains an attribute of Christ's visible, Catholic Church as she makes her pilgrim way through history.

[1] Further details in Ludwig von Hertling, "Communio und Primat", third reprint in the periodical *Una Sancta* 17 (1962): 91–125.

We cannot draw a clear distinction between the Christian's sanctification through baptism, Eucharist, prayer, the attempt to live out his faith—and the radiant example of those saints whose whole existence manifests something of the Church's innermost nature as the Lord's "spotless Bride". The notion of "heroic virtue" is more than misleading; it is meant to express the fact that a person has been so gripped by the love of God in the event of the cross that he can do things that, while they seem natural to him, are extravagant as far as the average observer is concerned. Such people have been gripped: that is the only reason why they make such vigorous efforts. They have been "sent", in a very special sense, for their mission has so taken possession of them that now they are nothing more than a function of the divine task. By calling such people God has in mind a particular fruitfulness in the Church—think of the great founders of religious orders—and this comes about if those concerned really take up the offer he makes to them. The task in view is never the person himself, but God's will, which he is to carry out. To that extent no saint can strive for his own holiness, for with all his strength he strains away from himself and seeks to enter more deeply into the will of God. It may be that God shows him the lukewarmness of the world as compared with the white-hot fire of love seen in the cross, and he throws himself heedlessly into the flames. He does immoderate penances which, for an ordinary Christian, would perhaps be irresponsible. The latter then speaks of "merits", of "works of supererogation" and "heroic virtue", and from his worm's-eye view he may be right. But the saint sees none of this; at most he sees how much remains to be done if he is to help to quench Christ's thirst for love.

There are always misunderstandings between the two approaches. The only question is: Which of the two sees things more objectively? The saint may be right at a more profound level, but the mediocre Christians are in the majority and so their theology becomes dominant. All the same, it has a hole in it: the saint is "canonized" and thus presented as a model to be imitated. But the average Christian cannot countenance a great vocation (which might lead him to similar "folly") and so, in order to blunt the call that comes to him from the "model", urging him at least to strive beyond his tepidity, he "venerates" the saint.

The Veneration of Saints

It is difficult to separate the element of folklore from the theological component. All religions exhibit the folklore aspect, the need for figures to mediate between us and what is ineffable, invisible, inaccessible. The depiction of the Mother and Child in Egyptian temples was spared by Christian Vandals. But has not the need for some visible response been satisfied by God himself in the Christian revelation? The *Pater immensae majestatis* is no longer remote: "He who sees me, sees the Father." And in putting on a pedestal our brothers and sisters who have responded to God better than we have, are we not engaging in a kind of idolatry that misconceives their whole cast of mind and their wishes in our regard? The seer of the Book of Revelation, sinking to his knees before the angel guiding him, is told: "You must not do that! I am a fellow servant with you and your brethren . . ." (Rev 19:10; 22:9). Of course, the Catholic makes a clear distinction between the worship of God alone and the veneration of the saints. But what, precisely, does he venerate? That is the theological question. God's presence, grace, his call, his victorious power demonstrated in a creature? In that case it would be worship, and worship of God alone, who, transcendent, is immanent in the world and the Church. Or does he venerate this person's response to grace and through grace? But if we distinguish man's response from the divine element in this way the notion of "veneration" seems questionable. If we reflect upon the Christ–Church relationship and the mystery of the *Sanctorum Communio*, this kind of sharp distinction falls to pieces. We worship the humanity of Christ because he is a divine Person. We do not worship the mystical Body of Christ, the Church: it is composed of created persons, albeit they are lifted beyond themselves and informed by a divine power which brings us close to the core of the mystery, the bridal union between God and humanity through Christ: *per ipsum et cum ipso et in ipso.*

If we were to venerate this mystery, the saints would have no objection, so to speak, to being venerated or honored. We would join them in gazing at the point that fascinates them, the point toward which, in self-forgetfulness, they transcend themselves. Far more is at stake here than feeling safe and protected by a powerful helper and advocate, feeling gratitude that the saint exists and admiration at his generosity: what is at issue here is the indivisibly theandric nature of the world, of which Christ is the radiant hub and the saints are those dedicated to him. Only in some such way as this can the veneration of ikons be justified: they refer not so much to the person depicted—Christ, angels, Mary, saints—as to the mystery that includes us, portrayed thus in archetypal situations and events. We look on from the periphery in veneration and longingly draw near to them in prayer.

For the rest, as far as the venerated saints themselves are concerned, we need not be surprised if they treat us with a certain element of humor. They will make light of the inevitable misunderstandings and, when we eventually see them face to face, refer us to the *Soli Deo Gloria.*

Quiet Miracles

The stories of Catholic saints are full of miracles, and there is no reason to doubt that a large percentage of them are genuine. The greatest and most authentic miracle is the saints themselves; the rest is a bonus. Handbooks of apologetics have hardly ever used the miracles of the saints to "prove" anything, as is (or at least was) the case with the miracles of Jesus.

We can surmise, however, that both the miracles of the saints and the miracles of Jesus were in the main (but not exclusively) quiet miracles. The biographers—and in the latter case the evangelists and their sources—turned up the volume *precisely because* they were miracles that only revealed their extraordinary quality after the event, when recounted to others. In many cases we can actually trace the subsequent heightening process. Who can tell whether the thousands who were fed in the wilderness only realized later that something strange must have been going on? The stubborn person will always be able to say it was coincidence that the Roman official's son was cured the moment Jesus said, "Your son is alive." And who can know—looking at things outside their revelation context—how much of Jesus' healing, his driving out of demons and his transfiguration was the product of parapsychological forces, and how much came from strictly supernatural causes? Or (another possibility) how much was a projection of the post-Easter experience on to an earlier time? At all events we cannot avoid the Johannine admonition of Jesus: "Believe me, that the Father is in me; or else believe me for the sake of the works themselves" (Jn 14:11; cf. 10:37f.).

We must not miss the kenotic element in the miracles of Jesus, and doubtless in innumerable miracles of the saints; the command to keep silence, emphasized so strongly in Mark, is certainly not some literary trick added later. It may be, however, that a "demonstration miracle" like the raising of Lazarus, which leads on directly to the Supreme Council's final death sentence, was intended by Jesus himself as a kind of introduction to his own dying and Resurrection.

In Christian terms it is right and proper that there should be places such as Lourdes where so much prayer goes on. But there too it is also right that the physical miracles (and how much more the moral miracles) should take place quietly and, as it were, "muted". They are not central: what is central is that thousands are granted the grace to pray and penetrate deeper into God's will, within a visible communion of saints who, at the same time, are sinners and sick people.

Mother Church

All the early centuries referred to the Church in this way. Luther still does here and there, but nowadays Protestants do not. Catholics are forgetting how to speak of Mother Church—at the same speed as they are banishing mariology. True, they still recognize the Church as a reality, but they are no longer prepared to be profoundly indebted to her. The *mysterium tremendum* of conceiving and giving birth has paled and become one physiological function among others; children no longer see why they should be grateful to their parents on account of such a chance act.

How simply, by contrast, the Church Fathers spoke of this reality! "Anyone who has not the Church for his Mother cannot have God for his Father." And as for our being conceived by God, which makes us children of God, it is by no means a chance act but the epitome of the freest, most creative grace. And for this act God chooses a womb. Just as he chose one particular womb in order to become man in a human way, so he chooses a womb in order to implant his life within us, in the Sacrament, which is Christ's presence in the Church. And the Church is guaranteed not only maternal fruitfulness, but maternal authority as well. The phrase that applies to Mary, *"prius concepit mente quam ventre"*, destroys every purely physiological idea of motherhood in favor of a view that takes account of the whole person: her whole being, from the apex of her spirit to the depths of her unconscious, says Yes to God's design. But in this she is only the highest instance of human fruitfulness, which, in the act of conceiving and giving birth, summons full human responsibility. And if men should forget this—with regard to the Church as well—there is still the boundless fatherhood of God to remind them of it.

All beginnings come from the Eternal Father; all authority, "authorship", *auctoritas*, in Heaven and earth comes from him. There is the authorship of the Son, eucharistically creating the Church and implanting his seed in her; there is that of the Church's officers, who are empowered to make this authorship present in ever-new ways in the Church as already constituted. This masculine activity would be impossible without the Church's prior, all-embracing, spiritual-corporal womb-quality. The individual receives Catholic grace from Christ, but he receives it through the Church and for the Church. We are born into the Church through Christ and the Church; the fruitfulness of both points back to the primal source of all fatherhood in Heaven. There can be no Catholicism without a sense of indebtedness. Jesus simultaneously acknowledges his debt to his heavenly Father and to his earthly Mother; the Christian confesses his indebtedness to the same Father who has given him the Son, and to the Church that is "one flesh" with her Bridegroom. But it is becoming increasingly difficult to put this in a way that can attract or elicit faith from today's monosexist man.

Apostolic

Scripture

The Word of God is not primarily Holy Scripture but Jesus Christ in the unity of his mortal and immortal, his personal and ecclesial existence. The Word of God is Christ, prepared for in the Old Covenant, acting among men, choosing the Twelve and other disciples, dying and rising again, sending his disciples out into the world and giving the Holy Spirit. This total picture is held fast in a corpus of writings that outwardly seems strangely fortuitous; yet, inwardly, its parts are seen to be related to one another in inexhaustibly new ways. As a picture, a form [*Gestalt*], it is open; as the testimony to the Word-made-man it is final and conclusive; thus it constantly invites new contemplation and interpretation. "Scripture" is rounded out into a unity by the Church in the process of establishing the "canon": the Spirit in the Church evaluates the Spirit in the testimony.

Scripture's inner unity far outweighs its outer unity. It outlines God's self-revelation in creation, dwelling cursorily at particular points in Israel's history. And while it does dwell on the figure of Jesus, it notes that "there are also many other things which Jesus did; were every one of them to be written, I suppose that the world itself could not contain the books that would be written." It goes on, then, to intone (as it were) the beginning of the Church's history, giving us an idea of its future course, and allows us a few glimpses through slits in the curtain covering the Last Things. Scripture has no intention of being exhaustive, Catholic; it is enough if the subject to which it witnesses is Catholic. It must be admitted that this subject is substantially contained in the letter of Scripture (as one of Quentin Latour's pastel sketches, for instance, captures the entire character of his model), in such a way that the Spirit-filled nature of this "sketch" suffices to keep all the legitimate and necessary further interpretations in the correct proportions. So the Spirit in Scripture goes beyond the letter, although it is not something beside or behind it.

Only on the basis of this paradox can Scripture be described as "sufficient", as the authentic document of a subject that far exceeds it, overflowing in all directions and swamping whatever we may deduce from the letter by the methods of philology. To that extent Origen is right when he says that Scripture is a "body" of the Logos and that the New Testament Scripture is a more spiritual body than that of the Old Covenant. Body is always the sphere of expression of a free spirit; while the latter may be bound to it for the purpose of self-expression, it can employ it in ever-new and different ways. All the more so if this "body", in its totality, is the result of the divine Logos taking material form. And even more so if this "body" is inseparable from the personal and "mystical" Body of the same Logos, inseparable from his eucharistic and bridal union with his Church, which "becomes one flesh with him" and recognizes him, fully and for the first time, only in this union. Now she realizes how much divine love is bestowed upon her through his "Body". (The husband embraces his wife, kisses her and makes her fruitful, using the same bodily members, but as long as love is alive it expresses something new, unpredictable and previously nonexistent each time, even if his wife knows all the time that "this and no one else is my husband". The Song of Songs is full of this constantly new realization.) Since all the experiences are new, we do not keep a tally of them. It is impossible to trace a straight line of doctrinal development through the Church's history, or a progressive unfolding of the "spiritual meaning of Scripture". Nor can we "add up" celebrations of the Eucharist; and Scripture can be only partially separated from the latter, for both look to eternal life for their complete, bridal unveiling. In the meantime they both come *from* tradition and contribute *to* it; they are determined by it in their very origins, and they have a shaping influence on it on the basis of those same origins.

The most painstaking exegesis is only objective provided that it takes account of this situation of the text on which it is working. Thus we can only call Scripture "Catholic" if it is embedded in the bridal ambience of Christ and the Church, in its unshakable faithfulness down through the ages (in the form of tradition), in the Church's missionary structure (i.e., its apostolicity).

Apostolicity

The Church is apostolic insofar as her government is entrusted to and exercised by the Twelve, guaranteeing an official structure and mission that endures through the ages and that can be verified, at all stages of her development, by reference to her primitive Christian origins.

Peter Brunner says, "Where necessary, the requirement of keeping the apostolic word takes precedence over the requirement to maintain communion with the Church's historical episcopate." But immediately he is obliged to add: "Christians are not in agreement as to what constitutes this normative apostolic word and the administration of sacraments arising from it. . . . That is why the churches are divided. . . . Dogmatically speaking, what is significant and serious are only the divisions which arise as to what is apostolic." But in that case, why tie the "apostolic" dimension to the word? Can we not say, on the basis of historical fact, that only the "historical episcopate" (substantially affirmed in common by the Catholic and Eastern Churches) is in a position to decide on this normative content? (Albeit it is the task of all members of the Church to live out this content in virtue of the charisms given to them.) Furthermore, it is the apostolic element of the Church that, historically, is the compiler of the Word in the form of Scripture. Only if we keep these relationships in mind can the Church remain *one*, as can be demonstrated both a priori and empirically; even where the apostolic reality lacks only one dimension—the Petrine—as in Orthodoxy, we can see its unity profoundly impaired.

Again, it is the charismatic dimension in all the members that shows and guarantees the fullness of apostolicity; it would be meaningless, therefore, to reduce this to a *nuda successio*. All the same it remains a skeleton without which the Lord's "Body" cannot stand upright. It is not difficult to see that, when fully formed (including the Petrine element), it has a *servant* function: it presupposes and stimulates what seems to be its opposite, namely the plurality of missions, charisms, theological and spiritual movements in the Church. "And although there were so many, the net did not break." Without the net of apostolic structure, which is stretched to the limit by the richness and plurality found within the Church, the manifold gifts of the Spirit could not be held together. Indeed, without it, they could not even be grasped as the richness of the One.

Authority as Form and Content

Nothing is plainer, nothing is more evident, than that in the Catholic realm the authority exercised in the Church of the Word and Sacrament is both form and content. Indeed, it can only be "form" (the exercise of full official authority) because simultaneously it is "content" (Christ's authority, which comes from his Father, which he bequeaths to his disciples in clear words). Similarly, it can only be "content" (the proclaimed gospel) because at the same time it is the "form" of the Church, which authoritatively proclaims it.

Were this not the case, there would be an alienating gulf between the proclaimed content (Jesus Christ's message and the message concerning Jesus Christ) and the proclaiming Church. Either it would mean that what is proclaimed (redemption through the Son's perfect obedience unto death on the cross) is a historical, objectivized, archaeological fact people can "hold to be true" without inwardly participating in it, such that his obedience long ago makes us "free Christian men" today. Or it means that we imagine ourselves (in a Pietistic sense) to be sharing directly in the event of the cross, and so reduce the primal act of Christian obedience to the miniscule proportions of an anthropological "honesty" that "does justice to the facts".

Church authority, the obedient exercise of the fullness of power imparted by Jesus Christ and handed on by the Apostles (cf. the Pastoral Epistles), preserves the necessary distance in order to join us to Christ's work in a valid way. Thus we do not imagine ourselves to coincide with Christ and his redemptive act, but all the same we are those who obey with *his* obedience and thus are followers of him. Obeying within the Church, we preserve the servant's distance from the Lord of the Church, and at the same time the Lord calls us "not servants, but friends", because we have been initiated into the mystery of his loving obedience, which is the key to all the mysteries of God in Heaven and on earth.

When we confess our sins, we obediently submit to the fullness of power he has imparted to the Church, which, for her part, responds in pure obedience to his command to loose and bind. The two interact, with the result that we not only participate in the continuing influence of the cross but are drawn into the primal obedience of Jesus' Catholic, all-embracing confession of sin on the cross and the Catholic, all-embracing absolution of Easter.

This is not blind obedience. As believers we know about the meaning and fruitfulness of the Lord's obedience, we know about his handing on of full authority and about its uninterrupted exercise down through the centuries. A person who believes in the fullness of Christ's power sees no problem in his handing it on. Indeed, the presence of this fullness of power in today's Church will be a guarantee to him of his Lord's living presence, even if he does not hear the echo, in the eternal realm, of what is done on earth with this full authority, and so remains one who "obeys" in the strict sense.

The Petrine Element

Notwithstanding all the problems connected with the papacy throughout the history of the Church, two things speak in favor of its recognition within the *Communio Sanctorum* and its apostolicity.

In the first place (and we have already touched upon this) the Petrine element is taken for granted, so to speak, right at the beginning, in the Petrine texts of the New Testament. And of these the most impressive is not the passage in Matthew but rather the overpowering apotheosis of Peter at the end of John's Gospel of love, which begins with the choosing of Peter in the first chapter and contains, at its center, the Apostle's great confession of faith in the Lord.

The Lukan text, in which Peter is commissioned to strengthen his brethren, is no less striking than the passage in Matthew. Then there are the very many other places in Gospels, letters, and in the Acts of the Apostles. How can anyone who claims to adhere to the Word—the Word alone—fail to be profoundly struck by these texts? In addition there is the fact that, since the first and second centuries, an undisputed primacy of the Apostolic See has been attributed to the Bishop of the Roman community. Rome had no need to demand to be recognized; rather, it was unquestioningly acknowledged, as we can see from the Letter of Clement, the Letter of Ignatius, from Irenaeus, from the sober Admonition to Pope Victor, etc. The principle of primacy had long been established by the time Rome allegedly began to put forward exaggerated claims when starting to develop its own theology of primacy. There can be many differing views as to when these increasing claims began to be unevangelical and intolerable within the context of the Church—in the fourth or ninth or twelfth century—but the "unhappy fact" had already taken place. One can only try to restore an internal balance within the Church, as the Second Vatican Council saw its task to be; it is impossible to abolish the principle without truncating the gospel itself.

The second argument for the Petrine principle is the qualitative difference between the unity of life and doctrine within the "Roman" Catholic

Church and the unity that exists within all other Christian communions. For, if we begin with the Orthodox, no ecumenical council has been able to unite them since their separation from Rome. And if we turn to the innumerable ecclesial communities that arose from the Reformation and subsequently, even though they are members of the World Council of Churches, they have scarcely managed to get any further than a "convergence" toward unity. And this unity, as we see ever more clearly, remains an eschatological ideal. Christ, however, wanted more for his Church than this.

If we look only from the outside, the Petrine principle is the sole or the decisive principle of unity in the Catholica. Above it is the principle of the pneumatic and eucharistic Christ and his ever-living presence through the apostolic element, i.e., sacramental office, fully empowered to make Christ present, and tradition, actualizing what is testified to in Scripture. Above it, too, is the *Sanctorum Communio*, the *Ecclesia immaculata*, concretely symbolized by the Lord's handmaid who utters her *Fiat*. But these deeper principles could not exercise their unity-creating power right to the end without the external reference-point of the Roman bishop. And the more worldwide the Church becomes, the more threatened she is in the modern states with their fascism of the right and of the left, the more she is called upon to incarnate herself in the most diverse, non-Mediterranean cultures, and the wider theological and episcopal pluralism she contains, the more indispensable this reference-point becomes. Anyone who denies this is either a fanatic or an irrational sentimentalist.

Dogma

Fundamentally there is only one single dogma, just as the human being is a single unity in spite of his many organs, conditions and views. This dogma is identical with the apostolic proclamation: He who rose from the dead has suffered on the cross "for us and for many"; therefore he is the Son of God; therefore he was born of the Virgin; therefore he is the Judge of the living and of the dead who will rise. And since he is God's Son, he is not subordinate to God the Father, and the Spirit he sent to his Church is really the Spirit of God, the Spirit of Father and Son. . . . These affirmations are not juxtaposed: they are interrelated; if Jesus is risen from the dead (and "otherwise our faith is in vain"), they logically imply each other.

The one, original dogma, the fact established by God, is the Catholic truth. Unfolding all that is implicit within it, we can show that it contains all truth necessary for salvation, from the meaning of the creation of the world to its fulfillment. The majority of the aspects of dogma are not deduced by merely rational processes; they are simultaneously read off from one aspect of God's self-revelation in Jesus Christ as shown in Scripture. Looking at the central fact—the Resurrection of the man Jesus, his saving death, his divine quality—our gaze opens out on both sides: to God, in whom the mystery of the Trinity shines forth, and to the Church and the world, which are given meaning in the light of that fact. With this twofold openness dogma embraces all reality: it is Catholic. We could also say it is maximal and thus contains the proof of its own truth and refutes any other truth that would claim catholicity, showing it to lack an aspect of the all-embracing truth. A loss of weight, of volume, has occurred, and this loss has an immediate effect throughout the totality (catholicity) of truth. If the Son is no longer equal in nature with the Father, as Arius asserted, but is only similar to him, the whole internal logic of the world's redemption falls apart, bringing with it the structure of the Trinity, the Church, and of eschatology, as the Fathers never tired of demonstrating.

Either the truth of revelation is Catholic, all-embracing, "greater than which nothing can be conceived", or it is not truth at all. And it is only in order to protect truth's catholicity against falsification and loss of substance that, down through the ages, councils have made statements designed to prevent the Church from veering to left or right of a proper understanding. There are three aspects to these so-called "definitions": (1) a form of words that (2) expresses a particular intention. (The words can be changed from time to time in order to bring out the intention in bolder relief.) In turn, (3) the intention aims at protecting the mystery which is the object of faith, which is not totally accessible to reason. This is possible because human reason can always see if some assertion curtails the totality or catholicity of the mystery. Thus the definitions surround the mystery like cherubs armed with swords of flame.

Sacramental Authority and "Infallibility"

"Lo, I am with you always, to the close of the age." The "chief Shepherd" (1 Pet 5:4) will guide his flock to its destination through the vicissitudes of the times. There will be nothing triumphalist about this, of course; following him, his flock will be privileged to walk along a "way of the cross", but in addition they will involve themselves in much human folly and imprudence, they will succumb to many a temptation, suffer many a shameful setback, giving their opponents plenty of grounds for triumphal rejoicing.

However, since the Shepherd has promised and given his Spirit to his flock, the Spirit implants in it an instinct for the right path. "The sheep follow him, for they know his voice; but they do not follow a stranger." This applies to the Church as a whole; but since shepherds have been appointed in the Church with the task of pasturing the lambs of Jesus, specially equipped by the Holy Spirit with the charisma of their office—"Take heed to yourselves and to all the flock, in which the Holy Spirit has made you guardians, to feed the church of the Lord" (Acts 20:28)—it is natural for the bearers of this office to have their particular share in the Chief Shepherd's guiding of his flock. This is not something exclusive, for the Holy Spirit is guaranteed to the entire Christian people (1 Jn 2:20, 27); they must keep in touch with the authentic instinct of the faithful. Similarly, the very center of sacramental authority, the Bishop of Rome, will not make his definitive decisions without consulting his colleagues in office and, through them, being in accord with the sense of faith of the whole people, particularly in the case of solemn definitions indicating a direction to be taken by all and binding on the consciences of the faithful.

Where does infallibility reside? Not primarily in the words or statements, for words can be changed in order to express an intention more precisely. So infallibility resides in the intention that addresses the mystery. The mystery, however, is an indivisible whole, whereas the intention can only address some partial aspect. Thus the formulated intentions can be seen in other, larger contexts; while this does not suspend them, it does relativize them.

What has once been discerned remains, but it can receive less emphasis when seen within a more all-embracing context.

The History of Doctrine
and the History of the Church

I mean the monstrous wars about small points of theology, the earthquakes of emotion about a gesture or a word. It was only a matter of an inch; but an inch is everything when you are balancing. The Church could not afford to swerve a hair's breadth on some things if she was to continue her great and daring experiment of the irregular equilibrium. Once let one idea become less powerful and some other idea would become too powerful. It was no flock of sheep the Christian shepherd was leading, but a herd of bulls and tigers, of terrible ideals and devouring doctrines, each one of them strong enough to turn to a false religion and lay waste the world. Remember that the Church went in specifically for dangerous ideas; she was a lion tamer. The idea of birth through a Holy Spirit, of the death of a divine being, of the forgiveness of sins, or the fulfilment of prophecies, are ideas which, anyone can see, need but a touch to turn them into something blasphemous or ferocious. . . . If some small mistake were made in doctrine, huge blunders might be made in human happiness. A sentence phrased wrong about the nature of symbolism would have broken all the best statues in Europe. A slip in the definitions might stop all the dances; might wither all the Christmas trees or break all the Easter eggs. . . .

The Church in its early days went fierce and fast with any warhorse; yet it is utterly unhistoric to say that she merely went mad along one idea, like a vulgar fanaticism. She swerved to left and right, so exactly as to avoid enormous obstacles. She left on one hand the huge bulk of Arianism, buttressed by all the worldly powers to make Christianity too worldly. The next instant she was swerving to avoid an orientalism, which would have made it too unworldly. . . . It is easy to be a madman: it is easy to be a heretic. It is always easy to let the age have its head; the difficult thing is to keep one's own. It is always easy to be a modernist; as it is easy to be a snob. To have fallen into any of those open traps of error and exaggeration which fashion after fashion and sect after sect set along the historic path of Christendom—that would indeed have been simple. It is always simple to fall; there are an infinity of angles at which one falls, only one at which one stands. To have fallen into any one of the fads from Gnosticism to Christian Science would indeed have been obvious and tame. But to have avoided them all has been one whirling adventure; and in my vision the heavenly chariot flies thundering through the ages, the dull heresies sprawling and prostrate, the wild truth reeling but erect.

(Chesterton, *Orthodoxy*)

Incarnatus Est

Destination World

Religion is the world in its journey toward God. Christianity is God journeying toward the world, and people who believe in him taking the same direction as he. Catholicism is Christianity which, with utmost seriousness, allows God in his fullness, the whole God, to pursue this destination right up to the bitter end—and ultimately to the end of blessedness. The other forms of Christianity become anxious about this degree of radicality. At some point or other they come to a full stop; at the religious and sacral level (the Eastern Churches) or in a mixture of spiritualism, which remains in its lofty elevation about material things, and secularism, which refuses to accept God's sanctification of matter (like the churches of the Reformation). The sick, says Jesus, need a physician, and the physician is the last person to be prudish.

The other forms of Christianity are somehow ashamed of God for involving himself so deeply with Adam's clay, for getting his hands dirty. Many things are left to take their own course; much is left to the individual's conscience and opinion. He is supposed to submit himself "to the word", but for the most part this does not concern itself with detailed regulations. So the decisive factor is mostly the *Zeitgeist*, the trend of the times, which looks at things from a secularized standpoint. Should the Church really involve herself with questions of sexual ethics inside and outside marriage, questions of contraception and divorce? Should she seek a binding interpretation of the gospel's requirement of poverty? Or, stepping into the area of the *mysterium*, should she try to explain more precisely the real presence in the Eucharist or the Virgin Birth? Why not simply let such matters alone? Catholic ethics often seems so casuistic and petty compared with other Christian ethics, and Catholic dogmatics often seems so materialistic.

There were many genuinely petty inquiries in late Scholasticism, topics pursued out of a curiosity that was unworthy of the profundity of the mystery. No one today will want to revive them. And no one will want to defend many a distortion found in popular forms of devotion. But behind abuse there is often a good usage, preserving a reverence for the matter of which man is made and which he has to reckon with, the deep, vulnerable, and often humiliating mysteries of human bodiliness (which is inseparable from his spirit): "Do you not know that your body is a temple of the Holy Spirit within you . . . ? So glorify God in your body" (1 Cor 6:19f.). "For God's temple is holy, and that temple you are" (1 Cor 3:17).

In the biblical revelation the world is secularized only insofar as it is deprived of its own illusion of being divine. It is sacralized, however, insofar as the only God, holy and sacral, who has created it, chooses it for his dwelling place in a wholly new and intimate way. And he does this, not in a vague and general way, but individually and particularly. He does not give himself to be eaten and drunk in every meal of bread and wine, but within a particular action performed for a memorial of him. And when he becomes man in the Virgin's womb, this virginity no longer has a merely negative character: it is the symbol, nay more: it is the sacrament of man's fruitful total surrender, together with all his abilities, to the God who overshadows him. (And it is appropriately reverent, at least, to assume that this eschatologically valid sacrament of virginity is not robbed of its blossom, deflowered, by the birth of the Son of God.)

In this perspective both forms of life, virginity (and celibacy) and marriage, acquire a new dignity, but a dignity that anthropology cannot get within its sights. There can be conflicts regarding the regulation of marriage relationships and the great problems overpopulation poses for humanity, etc., and the theological evaluation of them, but Christian reflection must take account of both sides. Since the establishment of the covenant with Israel and a fortiori since the Incarnation of the Son of God and the institution of his Eucharist, sexual intercourse can only be interpreted—in a fully Christian sense—as a pointer to the "one flesh" that exists between Christ and Church, Heaven and earth. The more insignificant it becomes for the world, the more precious it is to Christians.

As far as material things are concerned, the Bible is by no means squeamish: the world has been given to man for his use. But he is to use it in gratitude to the Giver and act responsibly toward him. Today mankind is putting limitations on its use of the world out of fear; the Christian should observe these limitations out of a sense of accountability to God. Between the divinization and the secularization of matter there is a third, middle way, known only to the Christian because its terms are set by the Incarnation and God's incarnational way of working.

Upwards and Downwards

Modern man's relation to material things is governed by the triumphant sense of his spirit rising out of the evolution of life-forms. Everything mineral, vegetable and animal becomes a preparatory stage, an infrastructure for man. It is different from that of the ancient non–Christian religion and philosophies in that the spirit is no longer felt to be a stranger in the material world, from which it must flee. It is felt to be a product of it, its blossom and fruit, its quintessence, now authorized freely to do what it wishes with the unfree forms of life that precede it.

God, on the other hand, is Spirit, free from all evolution, and he chooses the descending path into matter, not only in order to meet man intimately and in his totality, but also in order to show him the full meaning of salvation that resides in man's relation to matter, namely, that souls are (defenselessly) open to one another in the medium of the senses; the fact that man is fettered to vulnerable, corruptible bodiliness is something crucifying and humiliating, but it also has something glorious in store, which will shine forth at the "resurrection of the flesh".

In his "kenosis" God shows man that, right from the outset, he (man) is constructed according to a kenotic principle. It is precisely in this self-emptying and poverty that he will become—and already is—rich and glorious.

Relics?

The saints genuinely transformed the bodies they inhabited into temples of God, not only because their bodies provided them with opportunities for penance, but also because they worshipped and glorified God with all their powers, including their physical powers and senses. Catholics are not wrong to preserve and reverence relics of the saints, which can be a compass for their own life's path, surrounded by mist as it often is.

Christ, however, left no relics behind. His entire humanity was consumed as a holocaust on the cross and carried back to God at his Resurrection. All he left us is his living Eucharist. It alone is our "Holy Land", which can be anywhere on earth. So the relics of the saints are entrusted to us only conditionally: they are more properly part of their resurrection reality and, like the Lord, they tell us not to hold on to them. At best they are a memento of the Spirit who indwelt them and who is as alive as ever in the Lord's Eucharist. For Christ does not live alone in his Church; he is accompanied by all the saints who fill Heaven, and will nevermore be separated from them.

Pilgrimages?

How human it is to want to overcome spatial distance, with all the effort it costs! How human to strive toward a fulfilling goal that not only brings earthly delight—for every proper pilgrimage church must have a proper inn next to it—but also brings God nearer! Is this an idea inherited from the Old Testament, where God dwelt in a temple? The

Jews were well aware that "Heaven and the highest Heaven cannot contain thee; how much less this house which I have built" (1 Kings 8:27). But although Jesus spoke of the unstable nature of the Temple and of worship "in spirit and in truth", he was never above going there again and again, both as a child and as an adult; he was not above singing the "psalms of ascent" to Jerusalem. Catholic shrines have the grace of sending pilgrims away with the certainty that this grace is not bound to any one place. Having established their credentials, they efface themselves. It is good for us that Christ came to us, and it is good for us that he returned to the Father, otherwise the Spirit would not have come.

Intercommunion—Interconfession

In Catholic terms, Eucharist and penance form a unity. Jesus "does penance" when washing his disciples' feet, before sharing the Last Supper with them. Thus it is impossible to consider intercommunion without first taking stock of "interconfession", and, for the Catholic, confession is linked to sacramental absolution and hence to the power and authority of imparting such absolution. At this point we can feel the healthy "materialism", the weighty substance, of the Eucharist and of all the sacraments, binding them to the earth. We sense their sober realism. (Even in an "ecumenical" penitential service the non-Catholic participants would have to recognize the authority to pronounce absolution that exists in the Catholic Church.)

Penance and marriage are the only sacraments that seem to use nothing material—water, bread, wine, oil. But having to go to a confessor, to confess one's sins and accept a penance, is material enough. One realizes what Pascal meant by "*s'abêtir*": one touches the wood of the cross, so to speak, and not only that but also the loneliness of the cross. But this is indispensable if one is to partake of the *miracle* of this sacrament, which puts us back into the communion of saints, the Catholic intercommunion. The very fact that my own lonely sin is handed over to someone else, and that we can both see it in the light of the reconciliation won by the cross, is something miraculous. It is even more miraculous that the person to whom this sin is confessed is empowered to wipe out all trace of the evil, like wiping a blackboard clean. Or is it like that? For behind both of us, priest and penitent, there stands the crucified Lord who carries away the sin—this reconciliation is an *opus operatum* —and the panorama is so wide that the Catholic does not know what to do: Should he give a curt acknowledgment of genuine gratitude and go home, leaving the Lord alone with his burden of sin, or offer himself to the Lord to help him carry the load? But how can he do this? What we call "satisfaction" is an expression of this embarrassment, this awkwardness (which, at best, is somewhat moving) which can only say, "Thank you", and would like to say more.

If the confessor is a saint, a John Vianney or a Francis Xavier, he can take over the penance himself and make the symbolic relationship into a real one. When Vianney was asked about his method, which caused even hardened sinners to melt, he replied, "My recipe is to give sinners a little penance and do the rest myself." And if a priest complained that his congregation was lukewarm, the saint would ask, "Have you merely preached, merely prayed? Have you fasted as well, and slept on a hard bed? Have you used the discipline?" Here penance is seen as something that abolishes isolation by inserting the penitent into the communion of saints, which in turn is founded on the lonely penance of the cross. Vianney saw confessed sins only with God's eyes; so too he practiced penance not as his own work, but as a minimal participation in Christ's penance. Such "minimal" sharing was only right and proper.

On the basis of this realism the realism of the Eucharist becomes plainer. We can grasp its effect (provided we are ready for discipleship) and understand its demands (if we believe in its efficacy).

Celibacy

The objection to the Catholic priest's celibacy is that it is very difficult to maintain. The spiritual resolve has to descend again and again into the rebellious body and become incarnate. Day by day, year by year, the decision to follow the virginal Christ, to cling to the equally virginal (and hence maternal) Church, must show itself stronger than the most plausible objections of sensual man. This is truly a following of Christ in the act of incarnation, and hence also a following of the "lowly handmaid" who, right down to her least spiritual faculties, is at God's disposal and is rendered fruitful by him. And as for celibacy's aspect of "rule", it is this: a person is *privileged* to make an irrevocable decision to follow Christ, just as the Son's choosing to become incarnate remains irrevocable.

Religious Vows

Why not live out Christian poverty in one's own creative way rather than having to give account, in a petty and infantile manner, of every penny spent? (Answer: because the penny no longer belongs to me.) Why not understand obedience in a broader sense, as a pneumatic obedience in each new "situation", which cannot be codified, and in which God challenges me individually, rather than obeying another human being? For the latter may have no understanding of "my" situation, may be unable to read the "signs of the times" and may put me in a place where I cannot fully develop the best gifts God has given me. How many missed opportunities there have been for building up the Kingdom of God! *Ut quid perditio ista?* (Mk 14:4). And should not virginity be able to surrender itself if confronted with the more profound self-giving presented in marriage? Why this self-preservation at all costs? (Answer: because I have laid my spirit and my flesh on the altar to be consumed in the flames; I have no right to pull them out of the fire.) Catholic fruitfulness lies in the definitive act of the Incarnation, and its seal is what we call "institution". And the "divine fragrance" that ascends from the sacrifice is not my own spirit, emerging from experience, strengthened and transformed by the process of purification, but the Holy Spirit. It is not the superior who "sacrifices", but the one who obeys, and the superior must cultivate a twofold obedience in himself. And as to the mode of fruitfulness of the one who obeys, whether it be the invisible obedience of attitude or the obedience that is visible in particular acts, that is for God alone to determine.

In Jesus Christ, God has engraved his name upon matter; he has inscribed it so deeply that it cannot be erased, for matter (as matrix and *Mater*) took him into its innermost self.

It was surely a Catholic instinct that caused Christian generations to cut their name in stone, building huge cathedrals that, with their immense prodigality, mock modern man's obsession with utility.

But it would be even more Catholic if Christians tried to inscribe the name of Jesus Christ into the formless matter of human society, even at the risk of seeing the inscription dissipate in its ceaseless swell.

Ecumenism

A Definition

The Catholic who understands what being a Catholic means has no need to act in a specially "ecumenical" way. He *is* ecumenical because he is Catholic. The Catholic Church is not one church among others, she is the single source from which they have come, the point of convergence of all the churches that have split off from her. Only when joined to the Catholic Church can they plunge into the ocean of eternity.

As we have already seen, the Church's paradox is that it has a form and yet transcends it. For as a missionary Church it is essentially journeying toward the world's redemption, which has already been achieved in Jesus Christ.

However, this mission is a participation in the mission of Jesus, and as such there is nothing incidental or optional about it (as if "anonymous Christianity" were as good as the open profession of Christian faith). The person privileged to share in Christ's radiance is more profoundly redeemed than the person who is merely the recipient of these radiant beams.

It is surely not right to say that the Church will not achieve "extensive catholicity" until the last man enters her because only then will her dynamic mission be fulfilled and have become coextensive with its essential structure (C. Journet). Millions have already died without having encountered the Church or paid any attention to her. And when the Kingdom comes to subject everything in Heaven and earth to its head, Christ, the Church's earthly form will already have been sublimated in this Kingdom.

Thus the Church's earthly mission will not be accomplished in any other way than the earthly mission of Jesus, i.e., in the proclamation of the good news to those with open ears, those hard of hearing, and those who are completely deaf. In other words, the Church's mission will have to experience the pain of rejection, both in individuals and in whole nations, and this suffering will be more fruitful for the world than are the Church's external undertakings. It is important for the Suffering Servant of Isaiah to be both things at once, the great Herald of the divine message (Is 42:1–4; 49:1, 6) and the great Sufferer on behalf of all (50:4–9; 52:13–53:12).

Mission in Crisis

On the stage of world history the positions seem to
be entrenched. Islam, Hinduism, and communism
seem to be practically impervious to conversion.
And the strange thing is that when Catholicism
comes to doubt that it can penetrate these areas, it
actually starts allowing them into its own realm.
Its trinitarian concept of God is liberalized and
becomes a mere Deism and a belief in providence;
it dabbles in Zen meditation and (simultaneously)
in political theology. It is defeatism for Christians
to believe that the front lines have become fixed.

The Scattering

The Catholica seems destined to be plundered and
scattered. Throughout world history its members
and garments have been chopped up and ripped to
shreds. Everyone takes from it just what he can
grasp and no more; taking the whole would be too
much, too demanding.

Ultimately the Catholica looks like an empty
hulk (and not even a holy hulk!), a skeleton, a
framework, a carcass, while the living flesh has
been shared out among the denominations and
sects.

However, this is merely the way things look to
sociological observation. True, the Catholica is

bleeding from all her wounds, but in doing so she is following her Lord. She is more and more naked, increasingly without "form or comeliness", and her own sons begin to be ashamed of her.

The Catholica must not deny the scattered elements that are its own. It should be able to show that all these things are better maintained and integrated within its embrace rather than outside in the "diaspora". This would represent a common task for its saints and theologians.

Veiled Reality

Just as the man Jesus went veiled among men, the Catholica is veiled among the other historical constellations. Grace is required for a person to see through the figure of the Servant (and that of sin too) and discover the sublime reality beyond. "Flesh and blood has not revealed this to you." Simple people see this most easily, and the fact that sometimes they reach this discernment via folklore and sentimentality is irrelevant. Wise men too can discover it once they have been purified by renunciation and humiliation. The ones who cannot see are those who think they are so clever, the T.V. theologians, the sociological clerics, all those who think they can manipulate catholicity to make it more acceptable. But the *notae Ecclesiae* follow the Lord's footsteps into concealment; even in earlier times the fact that profane eyes *thought* they could discern these "notes" led to misunderstanding.

The Limitations of Our Age

Every age lives within its horizon and translates catholicity into its own terms. Let us not judge; our own age is limited enough. The Inquisition was one such translation. It aimed, whatever the cost, to protect the Whole (the "Catholic") from being dissipated into parts and by parties. The empires of Constantine and of Charlemagne were sincere and passionate attempts to incarnate the Kingdom of God; they were forms of political theology; and the reactions against this, from Hildebrand to Boniface, were an attempt to correct their one-sidedness (through others). If even the saints cannot entirely escape the limitations of the age in which they live, surely we cannot flatter ourselves that we can succeed in doing it.

Ecumenical Trust

Truths that are wrenched from the Catholica and live on in other denominations or sects often do so in a shrivelled form. It can be shown that they lack some contrasting and complementary element. But the ecumenically minded Catholic has no right to adopt a triumphalist pose, as if these truths can only develop to their proper fullness in his Church. Catholic truths have such vitality that, on occasion, they can unfold their authentic content even under considerable limitations, like strong plants in poor soil. This has been shown irrefutably by H.-E. Jaeger in his three-volume *Zeugnis für die Einheit. Geistliche Texte aus den Kirchen der Reformation: Luthertum, Calvinismus, Anglikanismus* (1970–1972).

This means that ecumenical debate is possible between the denominations without the Catholic having to relativize his standpoint, or rather that of his Church. Catholic truth can persist implicitly within the denominational horizon, within the denominations' explicit confessions of faith, which are often polemically opposed, since it transcends the formulas in which people try to confine it. Each dialogue partner can see the evidence of this in himself, and it can bring him to admit the same possibility in others. Each one has the opportunity of listening to his partner and adverting, in himself, to the difference between the formulation and what is meant by it (or at least to the difference between the formulation and the lived reality).

World Views

Something analogous must apply in the case of the dialogue between the Catholica and the great non-

Christian world views. The very fact that each endeavors to present a total interpretation of existence means that it is formally "catholic". The only exception is that of radical scepticism, and it too can be shown (as Augustine showed) to be self-contradictory; it can teach us that every formulated teaching carries its treasures in earthen vessels. With regard to the formally "catholic" interpretations, the task must be to see which of them can actually demonstrate its formal universality in concrete terms. Does Buddhism do justice to individuality and the world's historical nature? Can communism make humanity happy (or only some abstract humanity in the future)? And so forth. What would become of the world in toto if this kind of formal catholicity were to win out?

Church and World

What is humanism without a divine norm above it? Yet even the existence of a divine norm did not restrain ancient people from profound inhumanity as long as God had not become man and presented him with the eternal standard, namely, sublimity in humility, ultimate heroism in absolute surrender. This light had radiated a genuine humanism far beyond the borders of the Catholica; but it was the Catholica that preserved and cultivated this light. In this way it was like unity's yeast, supranational and suprapolitical (by contrast with Islam, for instance), yet not vague and other-worldly but with a constant incarnational tendency. The fact that it is both at once, the world's unity and yet not of the world, is what makes it suspect and the object of hatred. And that, in turn, draws attention to it: if a thing attracts persecution, it must somehow be significant. Hatred can always turn into a covert curiosity, particularly if one's own reality proves increasingly disappointing. . . .

The more immense the concentrations of power become on earth as a result of technology, the more the Catholica will be exposed, stripped of power. This is the apocalyptic separation of spirits, the Dragon and the Lamb. In baffling simultaneity the last book of Holy Scripture consistently shows us persecution, seduction and destruction on earth, and in Heaven the triumphant rejoicing around the Lamb who stands on the throne "as though slain".